Teacher Josh

English Idioms

Definitions in English and Mandarin

英文成语手册

Josh Bobley

Peter A Bobley, Mingxia Ma and Patrick Carlson

Marshall Cavendish
Editions

Published by Marshall Cavendish Editions
An imprint of Marshall Cavendish International

A member of the
Times Publishing Group

Other Marshall Cavendish Offices:
Marshall Cavendish Corporation, 800 Westchester Ave, Suite N-641,
Rye Brook, NY 10573, USA • Marshall Cavendish International (Thailand)
Co Ltd, 253 Asoke, 16th Floor, Sukhumvit 21 Road, Klongtoey Nua, Wattana,
Bangkok 10110, Thailand. • Marshall Cavendish (Malaysia) Sdn Bhd, Times
Subang, Lot 46, Subang Hi-Tech Industrial Park, Batu Tiga, 40000 Shah Alam,
Selangor Darul Ehsan, Malaysia

National Library Board, Singapore Cataloguing in Publication Data

Name(s): Bobley, Josh. | Bobley, Peter A., author. | Ma, Mingxia, 1988-
translator. | Carlson, Patrick (Patrick W.), illustrator.
Title: Teacher Josh English idioms : with definitions in English and Chinese
= Ying wen cheng yu shou ce / Josh Bobley, Peter A Bobley, Mingxia Ma and
Patrick Carlson.
Description: Singapore : Marshall Cavendish Editions, [2020] | Includes index. |
In English and Chinese.
Identifier(s): OCN 1176175811 | ISBN 978-981-48-9338-1 (paperback)
Subject(s): LCSH: English language--Idioms. | English language--Textbooks for
foreign speakers--Chinese.
Classification: DDC 428.24951--dc23

Printed in Singapore

Introduction

Having taught English to thousands of students in Shanghai for many years, my priority has been teaching colloquial English — slang and phraseology used every day by native speakers. Formal grammar, proper pronunciation and excellent writing techniques are important, but from a practical point of view, familiarity with vernacular used by native speakers is indispensable. If one doesn't understand common expressions like "I'm zonked" or "It's no big deal" or "I want to make a lot of moolah," it hampers one's ability to communicate with English speakers.

Recently my uncle, Peter Bobley, a well-known New York entrepreneur, author and former book publisher, asked whether my students know English idioms. Do they understand the meaning of "cry uncle" or "everything but the kitchen sink?" I told him that for the most part, no. He suggested that we put together a compilation of English idioms for a Chinese audience. I thought that was a great idea, and the result is this book.

English idioms are spoken by millions of speakers around the world. Quite a few idioms and expressions were invented by New Yorkers, many by Jewish immigrants. For example, "There's a glitch in this computer program;" glitch, meaning "minor malfunction," comes from the Yiddish word, *gletshn*. And the word "klutz," as in "You're such a klutz," meaning "clumsy person," also derives from Yiddish. Since I was born and raised in New York, and considering the city's world influence, quite a few New York expressions have been included in this volume.

English idioms books abound, but *Teacher Josh English Idioms* is different; each entry is accompanied by a humorous illustration drawn by famous American cartoonist Patrick Carlson (a.k.a. Cartoonboy), and includes a detailed explanation in Chinese written by my colleague, Ms. Mingxia Ma (马铭霞), a graduate of Qingdao University and a prominent educator. Also included is access to audio recordings of me enunciating the idioms, along with sample sentences, edited by Al Campbell, to whom I am grateful. With this, I hope to encourage students to read aloud at home to perfect their pronunciation.

Ever heard of the idiom, "practice makes perfect" (熟能生巧)? It may be an exaggeration since true perfection is unobtainable, yet it's an important reminder that hard work pays off. When I began studying Mandarin years ago, I never dreamed I'd be able to converse effortlessly in that language with people in China. But I persevered and now in my older age, I feel thankful that I put in the hard work. I hope my students will study diligently too — slowly and steadily — and utilize their knowledge in ways to realize their dreams. As the famous ancient Greek storyteller, Aesop, once said, slow but sure wins the race!

Teacher Josh
Shanghai, 2020

In a pickle
陷入困境

He's in a pickle because he only has ten minutes
to clean the store before customers start arriving.

在客人到来之前，他只有十分钟打扫卫生，这让他陷入困境。

Teacher Josh

To be in a pickle means to be in a difficult position. The word "pickle" comes from the Dutch word "pekel" which referred to spiced vinegar, a preservative. It was later used to refer to preserved cucumbers. This idiom likens being caught in a dilemma with vegetables that are mixed up in a jar.

In a pickle 从字面上翻译为在泡菜里，其实这个词最早来自荷兰。荷兰语 pickle 指的是腌制醋，是一种防腐剂。泡菜一般放在罐子里的，各种蔬菜混在一起很难区分，而且盐卤本身很咸，并不很好受，所以词义延伸为乱七八糟，处境困难。

Bite off more than you can chew
贪多嚼不烂

He thought he could learn to ski in an hour, but he could barely get down the bunny slope; he bit off more than he could chew.

他以为一个小时能学会滑雪，可是他几乎不能从初级滑雪道上滑下来，他有点贪多嚼不烂。

扫码看视频
Scan for video

Teacher Josh This idiom, which means to take on more than you can handle, could have come from the 1800s, when tobacco chewing was common in America and chewers would bite off more tobacco than they could chew. Another theory is that it was used to describe those who stuffed their mouths with more food than they could swallow.

Bite off 意为"咬下"; chew 为"爵"的意思，习语的字面意思为"咬下的比所能爵的还多。"这个习语可以追溯到19世纪美国，当人们咀嚼烟草时，有时往嘴里放的超过他们的承受范围。有时也说孩子满嘴塞满食物不能下咽。现在指接受的任务超过自身的能力。

Chip off the old block
相貌品性酷似父亲（或母亲）的人

扫码看视频
Scan for video

I can hardly tell the difference between Tom and his father; he's a real chip off the old block.

我很难说出汤姆和他爸爸的不同，他们长得太像了。

Teacher Josh The idea behind this idiom is that a child looks or acts a lot like his or her father or mother. It is said to have been first used by the Greek poet Theocritus in 270 B.C., to describe a piece of wood or stone that resembled the piece from which it was cut.

这个成语指某人在行为、外貌、爱好和性格方面与他的父亲（或母亲）很像。这个短语源自古希腊，block 指大块的木材或石头，如果从中切取一小部分称为 chip，这一小块和大的看上去也很像。同理，若把孩子比喻成小部分，家长比喻成大块部分，孩子在行为和相貌方面和家长很像。

Actions speak louder than words

事实胜于雄辩

That guy says he's going to give lots of money to charity, but so far, he hasn't given a dime. Actions speak louder than words!

那个人说他要给慈善团体捐助很多钱，但是到目前为止他连一毛钱都没有捐。事实胜于雄辩！

扫码看视频
Scan for video

Teacher Josh This idiom means that people's actions show their real intentions, not what they say. Some of the first variations of this saying are found in the Bible which teaches that people should show love by their actions and not just words.

这个成语有几百年历史了，最早在《圣经》一文中出现，讲述一个人强调说爱另一个人，但实际上不做任何彰显爱意的事情。美国林肯总统于1860年在库珀联合学院演讲中使用该成语，多指一个人做什么比说什么更重要，最好是做事而不只是说说。

At the drop of a hat

立刻，马上

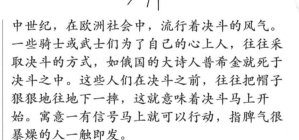

That dog is really annoying. It barks at the drop of a hat.

那只狗很讨厌，一看到人就马上喊叫。

扫码看视频
Scan for video

Teacher Josh This idiom means at once, without delay. It is said to come from the practice of waving a hat to mark the start of a race or fight. The phrase was further popularized in the mid-1950s when British entertainers Michael Flanders and Donald Swann named their debut album "At the Drop of a Hat."

中世纪，在欧洲社会中，流行着决斗的风气。一些骑士或武士们为了自己的心上人，往往采取决斗的方式，如俄国的大诗人普希金就死于决斗之中。这些人们在决斗之前，往往把帽子狠狠地往地下一摔，这就意味着决斗马上开始。寓意一有信号马上就可以行动，指脾气很暴燥的人一触即发。

Hit the sack

就寝；上床睡觉

扫码看视频
Scan for video

He was so exhausted that he hit the sack ten hours ago and is still asleep.

他太累了，所以他上床睡了十个小时后，现在还在熟睡。

Teacher Josh

To hit the sack means to go to sleep. This saying dates back to the late nineteenth century when beds were made of sacks stuffed with hay. Before going to sleep, people would literally hit the sacks to make them more comfortable and ensure there were no bugs inside.

古代，当人们上床睡觉时，他们会垫上干草，使床垫更舒适，并确保里面没有虫子，sack指装满干草的麻袋。二战期间，美国士兵也称睡袋为sack。Sack在俚语中指床，而hit是"打击、碰撞"的意思，但"hit the sack"可不是打床，一般指结束了一天的工作和学习之后，去上床睡觉。

Raining cats and dogs

倾盆大雨

扫码看视频
Scan for video

The storm was so bad, I had to run inside. It was raining cats and dogs.

暴风雨天气糟糕，所以我不得不避雨。外面下着倾盆大雨。

Teacher Josh While it is not possible for it to rain cats and dogs, this phrase is used to refer to heavy rain. Although we do not know its origins, this idiom is thought to date back to times when heavy rain would wash rubbish — including dead cats and dogs on the streets — away.

这个习语来源不详，据说可能是几百年以前在英格兰，每逢下大雨，很多垃圾冲入道路下的排水沟，包括一些死掉的猫和狗。它们的尸体在街上随处可见，好像和雨一起从天而降。现多用来形容雨下的很大。

A penny for your thoughts

告诉我你在想什么

Noticing that Sam was in a pensive mood, Lily said, "A penny for your thoughts, Sam."

莉莉发现山姆情绪低落,便问道:"山姆,请告诉我你的想法。"

扫码看视频
Scan for video

Teacher Josh This phrase is used when someone looks lost in thought and you want to know what that person is thinking. It appears in Sir Thomas More's book, *Four Last Things* (1522), where an intelligent man keeps his wisdom to himself and the townspeople offer him money to share his thoughts.

这个成语来源于Thomas More出版的书籍《Four Last Things》,书中讲述了对死亡、上帝和精神疾病的沉思,其中有一篇文章使用这个成语用来描述一种情形,城镇中有一位非常有智慧的男士,村民很想知道他是怎么想的,乡亲们甚至愿意付费给他。那时候一便士值很多钱。如果你想知道某人在想什么,你会乐意付巨额费用给他们。

Get in on the ground floor

早期入股;及早下手

Tom got in on the ground floor by buying Apple stock when Apple first went public.

当苹果公司刚上市,汤姆便及早下手购买股票。

扫码看视频
Scan for video

Teacher Josh This idiom means to take part in an enterprise from the start and thereby gain advantage. It is often used with reference to new investments, and probably originated in the financial world in the late nineteenth century.

"Get in on the ground floor"这个习语可能来源于19世纪的美国金融圈,通常指商人和企业家在公司发展初期投资入股,然后获得巨大成功,通常指进行新的投资。

The ball is in your court
决定权在你

扫码看视频
Scan for video

Whether or not you respond is up to you; the ball is in your court.

要不要回复，决定权在你手里。

Teacher Josh This idiom means that it is now one's turn to make a decision. While it is said that the phrase was first coined in the twentieth century by someone with a sporting background, views differ on whether it comes from tennis or basketball.

The ball is in your court 字面意思是球到你的场地上了，需要马上作出反应。很显然，这个习语是来自体育界，关于是来自网球界还是篮球界有争议。不管来自哪个领域，首次使用是在20世纪。美国的生意人和律师经常用这个习语来告诉对方，他们已经提出建议，现在是对方做决定的时候了。

A diamond in the rough
未经雕琢的钻石；璞玉

Her singing voice is unique, but she still needs practice. She's a diamond in the rough.

她的唱歌声音非常独一无二，但是她还需要练习。她是一块未经雕琢的璞玉。

扫码看视频
Scan for video

Teacher Josh This phrase refers to a person or an item that has good qualities, but requires refining. A similar term was used in John Fletcher's play, *A Wife for a Month* (1624), where the character was described as being "very honest, and will be as hard to cut as a rough diamond."

Diamond 指钻石，rough 意思是粗糙的，未经雕琢的。这个成语字面意思是指一颗未经雕琢的钻石，最初指那些没有经过雕琢的，特别是那些可能被打造成高贵珠宝的宝石。现在也用来形容那些非常有潜力的人和物品。

扫码看视频
Scan for video

Fit as a fiddle
身体健康

She practices gymnastics six hours every day and is in great shape. She's fit as a fiddle.

她每天坚持锻炼体操六个小时，体型很棒，身体健康。

Teacher Josh This phrase literally means, "in just as good condition as a fine-tuned violin." It is used to describe someone who keeps himself in good shape through proper exercise and diet.

Fit 指身体好，fiddle 是小提琴。一把好琴的弦和音调都很好，才可以弹出美妙的音乐。如果形容一个人 fit as a fiddle，是指这个人的身体状况很好。

All Greek to me
一窍不通

"This is all Greek to me," said Betty after being shown a technical document she couldn't understand.

贝蒂看了一份技术文件看不懂，于是她说："我对这些一窍不通。"

Teacher Josh This expression was coined by Shakespeare in *Julius Caesar*, where Casca uses it literally to describe a speech by Cicero deliberately given in Greek so that some would not understand it — "For mine own part, it was Greek to me." It was later used to refer to anything unintelligible.

这个表达是由莎士比亚创造的。在历史剧《凯撒大帝》中，古罗马著名演说家西塞罗在演讲，故意用希腊语说话，在当时，只有受过一定教育的人才懂希腊语，有一位叫卡斯卡的人没有听懂，他说道："听懂他言语的人时而相视一笑，时而摇头；但对我来说，却只是希腊语而已 — It was Greek to me。"很快这个词用来形容完全不懂，一窍不通，不知所云。

Put your money where your mouth is
说到做到

Jack put his money where his mouth is by betting Phil that the Yankees would beat the Astros.

杰克与菲尔用实际行动打赌，美国棒球队扬基队会打败阿童木队。

Teacher Josh This idiom first appeared in America in the 1930s. The idea behind it is that it is easier to talk about doing something rather than actually making the effort to do it. "Put up or shut up" is a synonymous expression.

中世纪，在欧洲社会中，流行着决斗的风气。一些骑士或武士们为了自己的心上人，往往采取决斗的方式，如俄国的大诗人普希金就死于决斗之中。这些人们在决斗之前，往往把帽子狠狠地往地下一摔，这就意味着决斗马上开始。寓意一有信号马上就可以行动，指脾气很暴燥的人一触即发。

A taste of your own medicine
以其人之道，还治其人之身

扫码看视频
Scan for video

I only pushed you because you pushed me first — it's a taste of your own medicine.

我推你因为你先推了我，这就叫以其人之道，还治其人之身。

Teacher Josh This idiom is taken from *Aesop's Fables* about a swindler who sells fake medicine, claiming that it can cure anything. When the swindler falls ill, he is given his own medicine, which he knows will not work. It implies that a victim may seek revenge using similar tactics on the person who has harmed him.

这个成语最早来源于伊索寓言，讲述了一个卖假药的骗子，声称可以治愈各种疾病，可是当他自己生病了，人们让他吃自己的药，但他知道这些药根本没用。成语用来比喻某人对一个人造成身心伤害，受伤的人也会用同样的方式抿复。

Bite the bullet
咬紧牙关应付

扫码看视频
Scan for video

Even though he hates needles, he decided he would bite the bullet and get his blood drawn.

尽管他很讨厌针，他还是决定咬紧牙关去抽血。

Teacher Josh This phrase is derived from a time when a patient would actually bite on a bullet to endure the pain from a surgical procedure done without anesthesia. Today, it describes someone doing something he has been reluctant to do.

Bite the bullet 这个习惯用语和打仗有关。据说过去战时治疗伤员的时候没有麻药，只好让他们咬着子弹，以此来应对手术的剧烈疼痛。因此，bite the bullet 意味着硬着头皮对付艰难情况，咬紧牙关应付。

14

Hold your tongue
别乱说话；保持缄默

扫码看视频
Scan for video

Alan doesn't speak freely to his boss for fear of insulting him. Usually he just holds his tongue.

艾伦害怕羞辱到他老板，所以不敢随便说话。通常他会保持缄默。

Teacher Josh This idiom means holding back from speaking, or refraining from saying something that might be insulting. It comes from the idea of holding the tongue between one's teeth to prevent oneself from speaking. This idiom dates back to the 1590s.

这个用语起源于16世纪90年代，话从口中说出来之前，将话语留在舌齿之间。现在多指别乱说话，防止惹怒听众。

Play it by ear
随机应变

扫码看视频
Scan for video

Joe was instructed to put all the bills in numerical order, but many documents have no numbers, so he'll just have to play it by ear.

乔被要求把所有账单按照号码顺序排好，但是很多没有号码，所以他不得不随机应变了。

Teacher Josh The phrase originates from the music world, referring to the playing of a composition without the aid of sheet music. A musician would simply use her ear to listen and feel out the composition. It now means to observe how a situation develops and make plans accordingly.

Play it by ear 最初起源和音乐有关。原来指弹奏曲子不用五线谱，音乐家靠耳朵去感受作曲，然后根据音乐随机弹奏。现在多指人们根据情形的变化相应地调整计划。

Smoking gun
犯错（或犯法的）证据

扫码看视频
Scan for video

She said she didn't touch the peanut butter but the smoking gun that proved she did was the fact that it was all over the table!

她说她没有碰花生酱，但是证据显示她做了，因为桌子上到处都是花生酱。

Teacher Josh This refers to something that serves as indisputable evidence or proof of an act, especially of a crime. The phrase is derived from finding a recently fired (hence smoking) gun on a suspect wanted for shooting someone. Such a discovery would serve as strong evidence that the suspect committed the crime.

该俚语起源于1970年代。刚射击过的枪，因为枪支内部发生爆炸，所以枪管一定会冒烟。如果某人被抓到时，手上正好拿着冒烟的枪，那他一定开过枪了，即"铁证如山"。所以 a smoking gun 不是冒烟的枪，而指的是确凿的证据，尤其指犯罪证据。

Beat around the bush
拐弯抹角

扫码看视频
Scan for video

He decided not to beat around the bush and, instead, just say, "I love you!"

他决定不拐弯抹角，相反，直接说 "我爱你。"

Teacher Josh This idiom means approaching or talking about something indirectly. It originated from hunting in medieval times, when hunters hired men to beat the area around bushes with sticks to flush out any game taking cover underneath.

Beat的意思指"打，敲击;"bush的意思是"灌木丛"。这句俚语字面意思是：绕着灌木丛敲击。据说以前的猎人为了把狼引出，故意用敲打灌木丛这种"旁敲侧击"的方式，来实现自己的目的。久而久之，beat around the bush意思逐渐演变为：兜圈子、绕弯子;说话拐弯抹角。

You can catch more flies with honey than with vinegar

对人要友善客气

扫码看视频
Scan for video

Knowing that you can catch more flies with honey than with vinegar, Janet brought cupcakes for the co-workers with whom she had been arguing.

知道用蜂蜜做诱饵比用醋能捉住更多的苍蝇，珍妮特送给和自己刚刚吵架的同事纸杯蛋糕来缓解关系。

Teacher Josh This idiom means it is easier to get something by being polite rather than by being rude. The idiom first appeared in G. Torriano's *Common Place of Italian Proverbs*, and later in Benjamin Franklin's *Poor Richard's Almanack* in 1744.

这个习语起源于意大利，但是现在主要在美国使用。美国第一次引用是本杰明·富兰克林在1744年《穷理查年鉴》中使用，引文是"Tart words make no friends: a spoonful of honey will catch more flies than a gallon of vinegar。"意思是：总说尖刻的话交不到朋友，盛满蜂蜜的汤匙比盛满醋的能捉到更多的苍蝇。寓意指：比起粗鲁对待，对人友善一些，更容易得到你想要的。

[Don't] Look a gift horse in the mouth

（不要）对别人送的礼物（或帮助）吹毛求疵

扫码看视频
Scan for video

Don't be disappointed. There's no reason to look a gift horse in the mouth.

不要失望。我们没有理由对别人送的礼物吹毛求疵。

Teacher Josh This means one should not be ungrateful when receiving a present. In the old days, when horses were sometimes presented as gifts, it was considered bad manners for the recepient to inspect the horse's mouth to see if it had bad teeth.

这是一个很老的俚语，在古代，马经常被用来做礼物，我们通过检查马的牙齿多少知道马的年龄。收到礼物后，如果你当面检查这匹马的牙齿，其实是很不礼貌的，这是对送礼物的人的一种不信任。尽管我们现在很少用马来作为礼物，但是这个俚语留下来了。寓意指，收到礼物后，即使不喜欢，也不要吹毛求疵，要感激对方的馈赠。有时也指接受别人帮助后，即使不满意，也不要吹毛求疵。

Pig out
大吃特吃

Bobby always goes overboard and pigs out at McDonald's.

博比总是很过火，在麦当劳大吃特吃。

扫码看视频
Scan for video

Teacher Josh This expression was first used in 1979. As pigs have a reputation for eating a lot, it has been common throughout history to compare a person who eats a large quantity of food to pigs.

这个俚语最早在1979年使用。因为猪有贪吃的嗜好，所以被授予贪吃者也不奇怪，将贪吃的人比喻成猪已经有很久的历史了。

Pardon my French
原谅我说粗话

Pardon my French, but you're an idiot.

原谅我说粗话，但是你真是一个傻瓜。

扫码看视频
Scan for video

Teacher Josh This expression is used when someone curses in conversation and may feel uneasy about using such language. It originated in the nineteenth century when English speakers would use French expressions and apologize for it if listeners were unfamiliar with the language.

这个词起源于19世纪，French是法语的意思，英法皇室联姻后，很多英国皇室一般只会说法语，老百姓看来，说法语是皇室优雅的象征。时不时在英语中加入一些法语，可以提升自身的品味。但毕竟掺入了外语，所以在说之前要抱歉一下。20世纪50年代，美国知识界很忌讳说脏话，一些会法语的人用法语代替英语骂人，认为这样礼貌一些，于是 Pardon my French 流行起来。现在指在使用粗俗禁止的语言前，请求对方原谅。

Clap back
以牙还牙

扫码看视频
Scan for video

She called him ugly names but wasn't expecting him to clap back.

她骂他，但是没有想到他会以牙还牙。

Teacher Josh This means responding to an insult or criticism, often with the intention to hurt the listener in return. It derives from the song "What Happened to That Boy" (2002), in which "clap" means "shoot."

Clap back 指的是对别人给予的侮辱和批评进行回应，有时以报复的方式回应。这个表达来源于一首歌 "Clap that Boy"，这里的 clap 指的是射击。

Cross that bridge when we come (get) to it
船到桥头自然直；到时候再说

When Judy asked her dad if she could go to Sarah's party on Saturday, her dad said, "We'll cross that bridge when we come to it."

当朱迪问她的父亲她是否可以参加莎拉周六的聚会，她的父亲说："到时候再说吧。"

扫码看视频
Scan for video

Teacher Josh This means to deal with a challenge as and when it arises, instead of worrying over a potential problem. The phrase likely dates to a time when crossing a bridge was a dangerous task due to its poor quality of construction.

中世纪，在欧洲社会中，流行着决斗的风气。一些骑士或武士们为了自己的心上人，往往采取决斗的方式，如俄国的大诗人普希金就死于决斗之中。这些人们在决斗之前，往往把帽子狠狠地往地下一摔，这就意味着决斗马上开始。寓意一有信号马上就可以行动，指脾气很暴躁的人一触即发。

People who live in glass houses shouldn't throw stones
勿道人之短

扫码看视频
Scan for video

You're too overweight to call me fat. People who live in glass houses shouldn't throw stones.

你自己都超重，还说我胖。勿道人之短。

Teacher Josh This means a person shouldn't criticize others when he has similar faults of his own. Its origin can be traced to Geoffrey Chaucer's *Troilus and Criseyde* (1385).

这个习语直译是住在玻璃屋里的人不要互相扔石头，意译指当自己也有相同的缺点时，不要去评论其他人。历史追溯至 Geoffrey Chaucer（乔叟）在1385年写的世界文学名著《楚勒斯与克里赛德》。1736年，本杰明·富兰克林写道"如果你自己家窗户是玻璃的，不要向你的邻居家扔石头。"这是博弈论的经典名言，指出于自身利益的考虑，双方都要维护一个互不伤害的底线。

Deafening silence
死亡般沉寂

扫码看视频
Scan for video

After living in New York City, the deafening silence of this country cabin is driving me crazy!

离开纽约后，乡村小舍的沉寂快把我逼疯了。

Teacher Josh In this phrase, "silence" refers to a lack of response or enthusiasm, while "deafening" implies that the silence is considered unpleasant. The above example implies that the person describing the silence misses the noise and excitement of the city.

Deafening 是震耳欲聋，silence 意思是沉默，所以 deafening silence 指的死一般沉寂，形容特别寂静，多使用在令人不愉快的情况。比如你发表一观点，然后周围其他人却没有回应的，大家都保持沉默，然后陷入沉寂，此时可以用 deafening silence。

Don't count your chickens until (before) they hatch
切勿高兴的太早

扫码看视频
Scan for video

He hasn't been offered a promotion, yet he's already buying a new car. He's counting his chickens before they hatch.

尽管他还没有得到提升，但是他已经购买一辆新车。他高兴的太早了。

Teacher Josh This is an old saying that means you shouldn't get your hopes up over something that has not happened yet because the outcome may be disappointing. It originated from Aesop, the Greek fable writer who lived from 620 B.C. to 560 B.C.

这是一个很老的说法，来源于古希蜡知名寓言作家伊索 (Aesop)，伊索生活在公元前620年至公元前560年。Don't count your chickens before they hatch 指的是不要依靠设想去实现愿望，结果很有可能会让你失望。

Give someone the cold shoulder
对人冷淡

扫码看视频
Scan for video

Steve gave Bill the cold shoulder, walking right past him instead of saying hello.

史蒂夫对比尔很冷淡，遇到了便径直走过去，也没有打招呼。

Teacher Josh This is used to describe somebody who is being intentionally unfriendly or ignoring another person. The term first appeared in the 1800s in a work by Sir Walter Scott, a famous Scottish novelist and playwright.

这个习语起源于18世纪早期。最早使用它的是瓦尔特·司各特 (Sir Walter Scott)，英国著名的历史小说家和诗人。这个习语的意思是故意忽视某人，对某人不友好。

Something smells fishy
值得怀疑

扫码看视频
Scan for video

Something's not right. It really smells fishy here.

有点不对劲，这件事值得怀疑。

Teacher Josh If a situation smells fishy to someone, it means she suspects something is not right or someone is being dishonest. This phrase originated in the early 1800s, referring to when a fishmonger was being dishonest about the freshness of his fish.

如果 smell fishy，你就要考虑有人不诚实，有些事不对劲。这个用语起源于18世纪早期，在海鲜市场上，如果一条鱼没有恶臭，那我们会认为这个鱼很新鲜。如果一条鱼闻起来有异味，说明鱼贩子骗人。现在多指某事或某人值得可疑。

Wolf in sheep's clothing
披着羊皮的狼

Bobby may seem nice on the surface, but he has a dark side. He's a wolf in sheep's clothing.

博比表面看上去很好，但他还有黑暗的一面。其实他是披着羊皮的狼。

扫码看视频
Scan for video

Teacher Josh This idiom is used in the Bible and as the premise of a tale in *Aesop's Fables*. It refers to a person with harmful intentions pretending to be a friend.

这个用语出自《圣经》，警示人们不要轻易相信一个看上去对你很友好的人。《伊索寓言》中也提及到，讲述了一个农夫被披着羊皮的狼欺骗的故事。Wolf in sheep's clothing 多指一位假装很好实际上很危险的人，一位假装朋友的敌人。

Charity begins at home
仁爱始于家

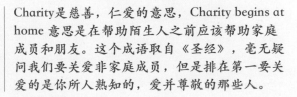

Henry believes he should help his wife and children before assisting others as charity begins at home.

亨利认为：在帮助其他人之前，他应该先帮助他的妻子和孩子，因为仁爱始于家。

扫码看视频
Scan for video

Teacher Josh This means one should care for one's own family and friends first before extending help to strangers. The idea that the welfare of those whom you know, love and respect should be a priority comes from the Bible.

Charity是慈善，仁爱的意思，Charity begins at home 意思是在帮助陌生人之前应该帮助家庭成员和朋友。这个成语取自《圣经》，毫无疑问我们要关爱非家庭成员，但是排在第一要关爱的是你所人熟知的，爱并尊敬的那些人。

Rule of thumb
经验法则

A good rule of thumb is to drink about one quart of water per day.

每天喝一夸脱水是一个好的经验法则。

Teacher Josh   A rule of thumb is a principle you use while engaging in a certain activity. The rule is usually developed through practice and is not precise, so it is treated as a helpful rough guide by many. For example: a good rule of thumb for staying healthy is to exercise twenty minutes daily.

Thumb是大拇指，rule是规则，A rule of thumb 意思是从事某项活动，反复实践从而得出做某事的一般规律，很多人会认为是有帮助的。尽管a rule of thumb不总是准确的，大部分时候是有用的。比如：每天锻炼身体二十分钟就是一个好的经验法则。

Pay through the nose
支付大笔钱

He had to pay through the nose to get that extraordinary car.

他必须支付一大笔钱才能得到那辆非凡的汽车。

Teacher Josh   This implies paying an exorbitant price for something. Its origin dates to the ninth century when the Danish levied a tax on the Irish. Anyone who failed to pay was punished by having his nose slit.

在9世纪，爱尔兰被丹麦人征服，需要缴纳很高的税，凡是被逮到逃税的人，鼻子就会被割掉。这个用语现在指为某物支付一大笔钱。

Dry run
排练

扫码看视频
Scan for video

Let's have one more dry run before the real show tonight.

在今晚真正演出之前，我们再排练一次。

Teacher Josh This idiom refers to any practice event in preparation for an actual event in the future. Years ago, fire departments in the US practiced putting out fires without using water. These rehearsals were known as "dry runs."

美国很多年前，消防部门在排练灭火的时候不使用水，这种不使用水的排练叫做"dry run"。现在多指事件在发生前的任何排练，做好准备，以防万一。

Tie the knot
结婚

扫码看视频
Scan for video

We congratulated Bob and Jane on tying the knot right after the wedding.

我们恭喜鲍勃和简在婚礼结束后结婚了。

Teacher Josh

This expression, which means to get married, has been associated with marriage since 1225. It is unclear whether it refers to an actual knot that gets tied during a wedding ceremony, or if it simply symbolises two people being bound together.

早在1225年，这个用语便和婚礼联系在一起，通常在婚礼中会使用绳结，婚礼中不一定要系绳结，但绳结代表的是将两个人联系在了一起，所以Tie the knot指结婚。

Clouds on the horizon

大难临头

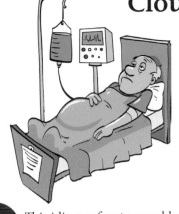

Results from the medical tests indicate there may be clouds on the horizon.

医学检查结果显示可能会大难临头。

扫码看视频
Scan for video

Teacher Josh This idiom refers to a problem that will likely occur. It is often used to describe a bleak economic condition, but it is also used in other situations. For example: "The driver didn't realize that the unusual noise from his vehicle was a cloud on the horizon." This implies the vehicle subsequently broke down.

这个用语经常用来形容经济惨淡，但是有时也会用在其他情况中，多指问题即将发生，尤指不好的事情。举例："The driver didn't realize the unusual noise from his vehicle was a cloud on the horizon。"（司机没有意识到他汽车发出的不同寻常噪音，要大难临头了。）

Let the cat out of the bag

泄漏秘密

He finally let the cat out of the bag and admitted he stole the watch.

他最终泄露秘密并承认他偷了手表。

扫码看视频
Scan for video

Teacher Josh This means to reveal a secret or disclose something that was previously not known publicly. It likens revealing a secret to letting out a cat that has been trapped in a bag; when the cat gets out, it can no longer be concealed, or made to return to the bag, again.

"Let the cat out of bag"字面意思翻译是让猫从袋子里跑出来，可以想象一只猫一旦从袋子里跑出来，绝对不会再回到那个袋子里，所以现在该习语多指原先隐藏的秘密被泄漏了。

Run like the wind

跑得飞快

扫码看视频
Scan for video

He covered a whole mile in four minutes; he runs like the wind.

他四分钟内跑了一英里。他跑得飞快。

Teacher Josh This means to run quickly. It appears in the form "swifter than the winds" in the Roman poet Virgil's work. Another old expression is "on the wings of the wind," which appears twice in the Book of Psalms.

这个用语指跑起来非常快。和他类似的表达有 "Swifter than the winds"。古罗马诗人维吉尔（Virgil）在诗篇中引用，后被很多作家使用。还有一个旧时类似表达是 "on the wings of the wind"，在圣经旧约书中提及两次，现在不太常用。

Doggie bag

打包袋

扫码看视频
Scan for video

She always takes home a doggie bag from restaurants so that she can have leftovers the next day.

她经常从餐厅打包食物回家，第二天她便可以吃之前的剩饭。

Teacher Josh This refers to taking away leftover food from a meal served in a restaurant. It is likely derived from the idea that instead of eating the leftover food, the diner intends to feed a pet dog with it.

A doggie bag 指的是去餐厅吃饭，将剩下的食物打包带回家的一个容器。这个用语为什么和狗有关系呢？人们委婉地说将剩下的食物带回家给宠物们吃，实际上自己吃。现在 a doggie bag 指的是打包袋。

Kick the bucket
死亡

扫码看视频
Scan for video

He kicked the bucket at age 50.

他50岁去世了。

Teacher Josh This idiom, which means "to die," has a disputed origin. It possibly refers to a person kicking away the bucket he stood on when committing suicide by hanging. Another possible origin is that "bucket" refers to a beam. As pigs would be suspended by their hind legs from a beam after being slaughtered, their legs would hit the beam, or bucket, when they died.

这个用语的起源有点争论：有人认为此用语和古代的吊死自杀有关，将死之人站到水桶上，等脖子穿过绳环后便一脚踢开水桶。另一种说法认为，bucket 指梁，杀猪的时候把猪的喉咙割破后，把猪挂在梁上，让他们失血而死，在死亡的过程中，猪会抽动而踢到这个梁。无论哪种解释，都指死亡。

Get a second wind
突然发力

扫码看视频
Scan for video

Though he was exhausted after ten rounds, the boxer got a second wind and knocked out his opponent.

尽管十个回合下来已经筋疲力尽，拳击手突然发力，将对手击倒。

Teacher Josh This idiom means getting renewed energy or enthusiasm after previously feeling tired or unproductive. Here, "wind" means breath. The idiom is based on the idea that one loses one's breath when fatigued (physically or mentally). When one can breathe well again, one becomes reinvigorated.

这个用语的意思是，当某人身心疲惫后，重新恢复精神，充满力量，当我们形容某人有 a second wind 的时候，这就是说他们疲惫之后恢复元气，又有精神了。

Get your act together

打起精神

His boss told him to get his act together or he'll be fired.

他老板要求他打起精神来，否则就解雇他。

扫码看视频
Scan for video

Teacher Josh This means changing your ways and organizing your life or work in a more productive fashion. It is believed to have originated in the theater industry, where actors feeling nervous or making mistakes were told to "get their act together."

这个习惯用语来自表演艺术，这是对演技差的演员说的话，意思是他必须把自己的表演提高到其他演员的水平，以便能配合共同演出。Get your act together 的意思可以延伸到生活领域，督促对方打起精神，努力上进，从而获得好的生活。

Hit the nail on the head

一针见血；正中要害

That editorial hit the nail on the head.

这条报刊评论一针见血。

扫码看视频
Scan for video

Teacher Josh With its origin in carpentry, this idiom refers to doing or saying something precisely right. In carpentry, if a nail is hit imprecisely, the wood might get damaged. Hitting the nail on the head perfectly, however, achieves the desired result.

Nail 是大头钉、图钉的意思，hit the nail on the head 可不是在脑袋上敲钉子的意思。这个用语指说话做事正中要害。它的起源和木匠有关。如果一个木匠敲钉子的时候定位不精确，就会损坏木头，敲钉子的时候得正敲在钉子头部才能钉准。所以当有人说话一针见血时，我们就会说他像敲钉子一样准。

It's always darkest before dawn
黎明前的黑暗

Things will get better. It's always darkest before dawn.

事情会越来越好。黎明前总是黑暗的。

扫码看视频
Scan for video

Teacher Josh This means things seem to worsen right before they improve. English theologian Thomas Fuller first used the expression in his work, *A Pisgah-Sight of Palestine and the Confines Thereof* (1650).

1650年，一位英国的神学家Thomas Fuller最早使用。这个用语的意思指在事情变好之前，看上去很糟糕。

Under the weather
感觉不舒服

扫码看视频
Scan for video

Maybe it was the seafood or maybe it's a cold, but Jim was feeling under the weather.

也许因为吃海鲜，也许因为感冒，吉姆感觉不舒服。

Teacher Josh To be under the weather means to feel ill. In olden times, when bad weather created rough sailing conditions, a seasick sailor would be sent below deck, away from inclement weather, to help in his recovery.

据说19世纪初，为了改善晕船情况，乘客通常会被送进甲板下的船舱里，可以抵御严酷的天气。故这个用语的意思是指生病了不舒服。

Rings a bell
似曾相识

扫码看视频
Scan for video

His name no longer rings a bell since he hasn't been on TV in years.

由于他很多年没有在电视上出现，他的名字已经不再似曾相识。

Teacher Josh To "ring a bell" is to bring up a memory of something. In a famous experiment, Russian physiologist Pavlov rang a bell when providing food to dogs. The dogs began to link the memories of tasty meals with the sounding of a bell, and would salivate when they heard the bell.

这个用语的意思是听起来很熟悉，尽管想不起很多细节。据说这个用语来源于俄国生理学家巴甫洛夫。实验中每次给狗送食物以前打开响起铃声，这样经过一段时间以后，铃声一响，狗就开始分泌唾液，准备吃食物。现在我们经常说"Does this ring a bell?"，意思是问有没有想起来？

Put your foot down
坚决反对

扫码看视频
Scan for video

Steve's mom put her foot down and demanded that he stay for dinner.

史蒂夫妈妈坚决反对，并且要求他留下来吃晚餐。

Teacher Josh This means to be firm and act decisively. When you tramp your foot on the ground, it demands attention. This expression's origins date to the eighteenth century.

这个用语在18世纪很流行，当你把脚踩到地面上，会引起某人的注意。实际意思指非常坚持，固执己见，坚决反对。

Throw a wrench in the works
阻挠；破坏

Bill threw a wrench in the works to take the ferry by announcing that he gets seasick.

比尔称自己晕船，破坏了大家乘坐轮船的计划。

扫码看视频
Scan for video

Teacher Josh This is a British phrase that originated in the Industrial Age (mid-1700s). It refers to disrupting a plan or project. If one dropped a wrench into the moving parts of a machine, or "the works," the machine would likely get jammed.

这个词源于英国，在工业革命时期，这个习语中的"the works"指的是机器，试想将一个wrench（扳手）扔到工作的机器里，很容易搞坏机器，从而影响工作的正常开展。现在指破坏或阻挠一个计划或项目。

Every dog has his (its) day
人人都有得意之时

扫码看视频
Scan for video

Jimmy has been down on his luck for years but won the lottery yesterday. Every dog has his day.

吉姆倒霉了很多年，但是昨天他中彩票了。每个人都会有得意之时。

Teacher Josh This means even someone less fortunate will have success at some point. Its origins date to 405 B.C., when the Greek playwright Euripides was killed by dogs set upon him by a rival. In the first century, the Greek biographer Plutarch wrote, "Even a dog gets his revenge."

这个用语来源和古希腊悲剧诗人欧里庇得斯（Euripides）的死亡有关系，大概在公元前405年，欧里庇得斯被敌人放的狗咬死。据记载在公元1世纪，希腊的传记作家普鲁塔克首次写"Even a dog gets his revenge。"这个用语的意思是指即使运气再不好的人也有成功的可能性。

Lend a hand
向…伸出援手

He's lending a hand to the blind man by helping him cross the street.

他向盲人伸出援手，帮助他穿过马路。

扫码看视频
Scan for video

Teacher Josh This common expression means to voluntarily assist. For example, if someone's arms are full of groceries, you may offer assistance in opening a door or carrying some items by asking, "May I give you a hand?"

这个用语指主动向别人提供援助。如果一个人手里拿着很多杂物，无法开门，你可以说"May I give you hand?"意思是需要我帮你开门吗？

Get out of hand
失去控制

A fight in a bar got out of hand and the police were called to control it.

酒吧里发生了一起打斗，已经失去控制，警察被叫来控制场面。

扫码看视频
Scan for video

Teacher Josh This means a situation is chaotic and uncontrollable. This idiom originates from an equestrian term used in Britain in the sixteenth century. If a rider did not hold on to the horse's reins correctly, the horse would go out of control.

这个用语的来源和骑马有关。16世纪英国流行骑马，如果一个骑马人没有正确地勒住缰绳，马就会失去控制。现在指事情变得混乱，失去控制。

Hold the cards
拥有掌控全局的一切

扫码看视频
Scan for video

What happens next depends on the President's decision. He holds all the cards.

接下来会发生什么取决于总统的决定。他拥有掌控全局的一切。

Teacher Josh You are in a good position to beat or defeat someone when you "hold all the cards" because you have the advantage. The phrase derives from card games and is based on the idea of someone holding the best cards.

这个用语的来源和打牌有关。打牌的时候，当一个人拥有最有价值的好牌，他便可以控制游戏。现喻指拥有掌控全局的一起，处于优势地位。

It is a poor workman who blames his tools

形容事情做不好的人只会怪别人，从不检讨自己

扫码看视频
Scan for video

It is not your hammer's fault that that window broke.
It is a poor workman who blames his tools.

你自己不小心把窗户砸破了，不是锤子质量差的过错。自己做
不好，只会怪别人，从不检讨自己。

Teacher Josh This expression describes someone who would not take responsibility for the faults in his work, blaming it instead on other factors like his equipment. Even with the best tools, someone without training cannot do skilled work.

这个用语的意思是指，在工作中如果没有做好，出现失误，一个好的工人不会责怪工作的工具，而是自己承担全部责任。一个人如果技能不好，即使使用最好的工具也不能做好工作。

Hang out your shingle
开小公司

A month after he graduated from law school he hung out his shingle.

从法律学校毕业一个月后，他开了一个公司。

扫码看视频
Scan for video

Teacher Josh This means to open a business. It is an American colloquialism that dates to the early 1800s, when businesses would use shingles for signboards.

Hang out your shingle指的是开一个公司。这个美国俗语起源于19世纪上半叶，最初是律师所营业要有牌照，后来扩展到医生和其他商业都要有营业牌照。

An ounce of prevention is worth a pound of cure
预防为主，治疗为辅

扫码看视频
Scan for video

Better put some air in that tire. An ounce of prevention is worth a pound of cure.

预防起见，最好往轮胎里打点气。

Teacher Josh This means taking precautions before a crisis occurs is preferable to fixing things afterwards. Benjamin Franklin first used the phrase in a letter to Philadelphia government officials, suggesting it would be less costly to prevent fires than deal with their consequences.

这个用语来源于本杰明·富兰克林，有一次他访问波士顿，这个城市的防火措施让他印象深刻，当他返回费城，他决定要提高自己居住城市的消防能力，于是便写信给当地的政府官员，信件中说"It would be less costly to prevent fires than dealing with their consequences。"（预防火灾的花费要比处理火灾的成本的低。）An ounce of prevention is worth a pound of cure指预防为主，治愈为辅。

Shoot the breeze

聊天，吹牛

Let's sit around and just shoot the breeze.

让我们坐下来聊聊天，吹吹牛。

Teacher Josh This idiom, which originated in the USA in the early 1900s, means to casually talk. A breeze, or a light wind, was at one time slang for a rumor.

这个用语最早起源于美国19世纪中期，breeze 是微风的意思，曾经是一个关于谣言的习语。

Dropping like flies

大批死亡；纷纷倒下

Everyone seems to be getting the flu. People are dropping like flies.

每个人看上去都感染了流感，一大批纷纷倒下死亡。

Teacher Josh This idiom, which means people are falling sick or dying in a large or growing group, is an allusion to the short lifespan of flies.

该习语暗指苍蝇短暂的生命周期，现多用来描述人们大规模的生病或死亡。

Like riding a bicycle (bike)
就像骑自行车（那么容易）

扫码看视频
Scan for video

It will come back to you; it's just like riding a bike.

你很快就掌握了，就像骑自行车一样。

Teacher Josh This means any skill once learned is never forgotten. Once a person learns to ride a bicycle, it is something she will always be able to do.

这个用语表达的意思是，有些技能，一旦掌握，便很难忘记，比如很多人不会忘记骑自行车。还有其他的一些技能，比如打棒球和投掷飞盘。

Take a hike
离开

扫码看视频
Scan for video

He wouldn't stop talking and it was annoying me,
so I told him to leave — to take a hike.

他不停地抱怨使我很烦，所以我让他离开了！

Teacher Josh

This phrase is usually told to someone annoying, to get the person to go away. While its origin is uncertain, the word "hyke," which means to take a vigorous walk, was first used in the early 1800s.

这个用语中的hike起源不是很明确，但是单词"hyke"在19世纪用过，意思是参加一次有活力的的徒步。到1830 年，hike 意思是粗鲁的告诉某人离开。Take a hike 是一个粗鲁的短语，多指让讨厌的人走开。

Costs an arm and a leg
非常昂贵

Man, that's expensive for a shirt. It costs an arm and a leg!

哇塞，这件T恤衫价值不菲。非常昂贵！

扫码看视频
Scan for video

Teacher Josh This expression describes something that's extremely expensive. It is uncertain where this phrase originated, but it may have come from the battlefield, where soldiers can easily lose a limb while fighting for their country.

这个习语用来形容某物很贵。没有人知道它的来源，但是有些人认为来自20世纪的世界大战。战争中的士兵，在一线作战很容易失去胳膊，所以战争很容易会夺走士兵的胳膊和腿，这是非常昂贵的代价。

The pot calling the kettle black
五十步笑百步

扫码看视频
Scan for video

You calling me crazy is ridiculous considering we're both crazy. It's the pot calling the kettle black!

你笑话我疯狂简直可笑，因为我们俩都很疯狂。真是五十步笑百步。

Teacher Josh This describes a situation when a person criticizes another for a fault that he also has. The saying is at least 400 years old and dates to a time when the bottom of kettles, like the bottom of pots, were black from being hung over a fire — thus the pot metaphorically accuses the kettle of the fault it shares.

习语中the pot 指锅，kettle 指壶，字面意思是锅嫌弃壶黑。很久以前，烧水和做饭都是将壶和锅放置到火上，时间久了铁就变黑了。这个习语至少有400年历史了，它用来讽刺别人自己也有同样的问题，却在抱怨或批评其他人。在现代英语中的含义和厨具并无关系，这个说法的意思和汉语里的俗语"五十步笑百步"、"半斤八两"有异曲同工之妙。

A chip on your shoulder

怀恨在心；愤愤不平

扫码看视频
Scan for video

She's been very bitter for a long time. She has a chip on her shoulder about her divorce twenty years ago.

她很长一段时间很尖刻。对于20年前的离婚，她怀恨在心。

Teacher Josh A person who has a chip on his shoulder is someone who feels wronged. This idiom originated in the USA in the nineteenth century, when a person wanting to get into a fight would carry a wood chip on his shoulder, daring others to knock it off.

用语起源于19世纪的美国，如果一个人想要和某人打斗，他会在自己的肩膀上放上一根木头（chip指的是木头），看对方是否敢把木头击倒。现在这个习语多用来描述一个人受到了委屈，然后怀恨在心，愤愤不平。

It's a piece of cake

易如反掌；小菜一碟

The test was particularly easy — a piece of cake.

这个测试特别简单，小菜一碟。

扫码看视频
Scan for video

Teacher Josh This means something easy to do. This term originated from a nineteenth century tradition of having enslaved African-Americans take part in a competition of dancing around a cake. The pair with the most graceful moves would win the cake as their prize From this also came the term "cakewalk," which likewise means something easily accomplished.

Cake 这个词怎么和简单联系在一起呢？这起源于19世纪70年代，当时如果赢得比赛，就会用蛋糕当作奖品。特别是在美国奴隶社会时期，有一个传统就是奴隶们在聚会上围着蛋糕组成圆圈跳舞，最优雅的舞伴会获得奖品，奖品就是蛋糕。自此以后，"cake walk"和"piece of cake"短语出现了，多指有些事特别简单去完成。

Break the ice
打破沉默

扫码看视频
Scan for video

Let's have a drink to get to know each other,
and break the ice.

让我们喝一杯多了解彼此，从而打破沉默。

Teacher Josh To break the ice is to get past the initial awkwardness when getting to know a new person. This phrase likely came from the practice of boats breaking the ice in the water to ensure a clear path of travel. It first appeared in *Hudibras*, a poem by Samuel Butler in the seventeenth century.

据史料记载，这个习语最早记录追溯到17世纪，出现在塞缪尔·巴特勒 (Samuel Butler) 写的诗中《胡迪布拉斯》(Hudibras)。最早应用在破冰船在冰冻海域进行破冰。现在多指和一个人第一次见面，打破僵局，避免尴尬。

Hang out

闲逛; 出去玩

扫码看视频
Scan for video

Let's spend the weekend together. We'll just hang out with no particular plan.

让我们周末一起聚一下吧。我们就是没有任何计划的闲逛而已。

Teacher Josh This means to spend time informally with others. The *Oxford English Dictionary* states that as early as 1846, this phrase has been used to mean often going to and spending time at a certain place, or spending time with people.

这个习语最早在1846年牛津英语词典中被引用，指去一个经常去的地方，比如说一个酒吧，也指人们聚在一起打磨时光。

I could eat a horse
我饿极了

I'm so hungry I could eat the entire buffet.
I could eat a horse!

我饿的能吃掉整个自助餐。我真是饿极了。

Teacher Josh This is used to mean that the speaker is extremely hungry. It shows that one is so hungry that in desperate need of a large quantity of food, one would even consider eating a horse. Although its origin is unknown, this phrase dates to the nineteenth century.

这个用语的起源不知道，但是从19世纪就开始使用了。这个用语从字面意思看，是指我可以吃掉一匹马。马是一个比较大的动物，能吃掉一匹马形容一个人太饿了。即使你不想吃，但是如果极度饥饿，你也会被迫选择吃掉它。

Ruffle feathers
激怒某人

I like him, but sometimes he gets on my nerves and ruffles my feathers.

我喜欢他，但是有时候他让我抓狂，惹恼并且激怒我。

Teacher Josh In use since the mid-1800s, this idiom means to annoy. It comes from the mistaken belief that when a bird is agitated or angry, the feathers around its neck would stand upright, making it look puffed up. However, birds ruffle their feathers for different reasons, such as to greet other birds or to keep warm.

从1800年开始，ruffle feathers 指的是一个鸟在颈部的羽毛直立起来并且张开。这个习语的起源来源于一个错误的认知，人们认为鸟颈部羽毛直立起来是因为烦躁生气。事实上，鸟直立羽毛有很多种原因，比如天气变暖、问候或者是生病了。现在多指激怒某人。

Hit the ceiling
勃然大怒

He hit the ceiling when he saw the damage they did to the carpet.

当他看到他们对地毯造成的损坏，他勃然大怒。

Teacher Josh Dating to the early 1900s, this idiom describes someone who loses his temper. A similar expression is "hit the roof."

这个习语起源于20世纪初，"hit the ceiling" 可不是撞击天花板的意思，实际意思是描述一个人非常生气，发脾气。近似的表达还有 "hit the roof"，都是形容一个人勃然大怒。

Spill the beans
泄露秘密

When the police questioned him, he told them what they wanted to know — he spilled the beans.

当警察质问他的时候，他告诉警察他们想知道的一切。他泄露秘密了。

Teacher Josh This means to reveal information that is supposed to be secret. In ancient Greece, there was a voting system involving placing beans in jars. White beans would indicate "yes" while black beans would mean "no." However, if a jar were accidentally knocked over during voting, the beans would spill out and the votes would become known.

在这个习语中，spill 是洒的意思，beans是豆子的意思。那 spill the beans就是豆子洒了吧？其实，这个习语真正的意思是泄漏秘密。在古希腊，有一个选举方法就是将对应的豆子投入罐子里，豆子有两种颜色，白色的豆子代表的是 yes，黑色的豆子代表的是 no。在选举结束之前，没有人知道每个罐子里有多少选票。这是个秘密。但是如果这个罐子被意外的撞倒了，里面的豆子撒了出来，那么选举的结果就暴露了。这就是这个习语的起源吧。

Keep me in the loop
有消息就通知我

扫码看视频
Scan for video

I'm very anxious to know what will happen, so please keep me in the loop.

我很渴望知道发生了什么，有消息就通知我。

Teacher Josh This is a request to be kept informed or updated about something. "Loop" refers to a closed circular shape. The phrase "in the loop" means someone, like everyone else in a group (or circle), is aware of a situation. This expression originated in the 1970s and may have been derived from computer terminology.

这个用语起源于1970年，有时候被认为是一种计算机术语。Loop这个词指一个圆圈或者是一个持续的循环的动作。Being in the loop 指的是你知道事情进展。Being kept in the loop 指请求别人及时通知你事情的进展。

A different kettle of fish
截然不同

扫码看视频
Scan for video

When speaking of tall persons, NBA players are of another league. They are a different kettle of fish.
说到身高，NBA的球员和在其他任何联盟不一样，是截然不同的。

Teacher Josh Originating in Scotland in 1785, this idiom is used to describe something that is different from another thing that had been mentioned. It means the two things cannot be compared as they are dissimilar.

这个用语起源于苏格兰，如果说某事是"a different kettle of fish"，指的是某事与你说的类似的事是截然不同的。

Hang in there
坚持下去

The pain will end soon. Stay calm. Hang in there!

痛苦很快就结束了。保持镇定。坚持下去。

扫码看视频
Scan for video

Teacher Josh This means to remain persistent and determined in difficult times. The phrase, which gained popularity when it was featured in an American poster in 1970s showing a cat hanging on a bamboo pole, is used to encourage those who are struggling.

这个习语是在1970年开始流行的，得益于一个流行的海报。这个海报精选了一只猫挂在一支竹杆上面，看上去卡在那里不能动了。现在多指的是在困难的情景下继续坚持下去。人们使用"hang in there"鼓励正在经受困境的人们。

Once in a blue moon
千载难逢

扫码看视频
Scan for video

The professor sets his students homework almost every night, but very rarely, once in a blue moon, he forgets.

教授每天晚上都布置家庭作业，这次很罕见，千载难逢，他忘记了。

Teacher Josh This phrase now means very rarely, but years ago it was used to describe something that seemed illogical and unlikely. Its first known recorded use was in a pamphlet published in 1528 that criticized the religious authorities.

Once in a blue moon很多年前是荒谬的意思，和习语"when pigs fly"意思差不多。最早记载，William Roy 和 Jeremy Barlowe 在1528年出版的反对教会权利的小册子中使用。"Once in a blue moon"，once是一次的意思，blue moon不是指蓝色的月亮，而是指"一个月中第二次满月"，这种情况很少见，大约每32个月左右会出现一次"一个月两次圆月"的现象。因此，once in a blue moon 现在多指很少发生的事情。

Burn bridges
破釜沉舟

She's fought with everyone in the office and will soon have no allies there. She's burning her bridges.

她和办公室里的每个人都打架了，很快没有同盟了。她破釜沉舟了。

扫码看视频
Scan for video

Teacher Josh When one burns bridges, one is doing something that cannot be reversed easily. It often refers to actions that lead to the fracturing of friendships and professional relations. This idiom comes from ancient Rome, when bridges were destroyed and boats burned during warfare. As such, "to burn one's boats" also has the same meaning.

这个用语起源于罗马。像很多习语一样，这些用语都有一个字面意思，在罗马战争中有个惯例就是摧毁桥。"To burn one's bridges"和"to burn one's boats"意思一样，指的是做了一件事情，想回复到从前很难了。

Sell like hotcakes
抢手货

LeBron jerseys are selling extremely well. They're selling like hotcakes.

印有勒布朗·詹姆斯的衬衫卖的特别好。它们是抢手货。

扫码看视频
Scan for video

Teacher Josh This means something is selling quickly and likely in huge quantity. Originating in the USA, where hotcakes are pancakes, the expression is believed to be derived from fairs and festivals, where hotcakes often sell out quickly.

该习语起源于美国，hotcake 一词于19世纪被发明，那时在集市或节日中比较受欢迎的是 pancake，pancake 就是 hotcake，所以 sell like hotcakes 指的就是产品很畅销，卖的很快，卖的很多。

Come out of your shell
不再害羞

扫码看视频
Scan for video

At first, John felt shy at the party, but once the music began, the true John emerged — he came out of his shell.
参加聚会约翰感觉害羞，但是当音乐一响起来，约翰回归自我，他不再害羞了。

Teacher Josh This describes someone who stops being shy and becomes more friendly and at ease with talking to others. The idiom alludes to a turtle emerging from its shell.

这个习语暗指害羞的乌龟从它的壳子里出来了。如果有人"comes out of his shell"，他便停止害羞和沉默寡言，变得更亲切，喜好社交的。

Rock the boat
捣乱；无事生非

扫码看视频
Scan for video

Bill's food truck had been a big success for years, so when he told his wife that he wanted to stop selling hamburgers and start selling dumplings she said, "Why rock the boat?"

比尔快餐车生意已经成功了很多年，当他告诉他的妻子他想要停止售卖汉堡包，要开始卖饺子，她妻子说："为什么无事生非？"

Teacher Josh This means to stir up trouble. It is attributed to American politician William Jennings Bryan, who in 1914 said: "The man who rocks the boat ought to be stoned when he gets back on shore."

这个习语来源于美国一位著名的政客和律师——威廉·詹宁斯·布赖恩。他在1914年引证中讲到"The man who rocks the boat ought to be stoned when he gets back on shore。"显然"rock the boat"这里的意思指的是那些捣乱分子，无事生非的人。

Steal someone's thunder
抢某人风头

扫码看视频
Scan for video

I didn't mean to steal your thunder — to mention your good news before you had the chance — but I told your dad that you were made Captain.

在你说出好消息前我已经帮你说了，我告诉你父亲你是队长，我并不是有意抢你风头。

Teacher Josh This means to take another person's idea as your own or carry out someone else's plan before they do for praise or your own benefit. In the early 1700s, English dramatist John Dennis conceived a way of producing thunder sounds for his unsuccessful play *Appius and Virginia*, only to later find it used in a production of Shakespeare's *Macbeth*. Thus, Dennis felt that his idea for making thunder had been stolen.

Steal 解释为"偷"，Thunder 是"雷电"，Steal thunder 指的是剽窃某人尚未发表的想法观点或发明创造，企图攫取他人的成果和荣誉。这一表达的背后有个小故事。1709年，剧作家John Dennis在他的新剧 Appius and Virginia 中使用了一种新方法制造雷声，没想到这个剧反响太差，以失败告终。但是后来，这种制造雷声的方法用在了 Shakespeare 四大悲剧之一的《麦克白》（Macbeth）中，John Dennis 就不开心了，觉得自己的 thunder 被 steal 了。

Bigger fish to fry
有更重要的事情去处理

扫码看视频
Scan for video

John asked Sally to help wash his car, but she said no because she had a more important date. She had bigger fish to fry.

约翰请求莎莉帮忙洗车，但是她拒绝了，因为她有一个更重要的约会。她有更重要的事情去处理。

Teacher Josh This means one has more important matters to attend to. It appears in an English translation of *Don Quixote*, a Spanish novel published in the early 1600s. However, the idiom could be older as other languages have similar sayings. For instance, the French have: "There are other dogs to whip."

这个用语首次使用已经超过 400 年了，可能更早。有线索显示几百万年前在其他语言中有类似的表达，比如在西班牙小说《唐·吉诃德》的首次英文翻译中出现过。在法语语言中有一个相似的表达："other dogs to whip（鞭打其他的狗）"。

It takes one to know one
彼此彼此

One robber said to the other that it takes one to know one, because they were both bad guys.

一个盗贼对另一个人说彼此彼此，因为他们都是坏家伙。

扫码看视频
Scan for video

Teacher Josh This idiom describes how people who behave in certain ways or have certain character traits are often better at recognizing similar characteristics in others. It dates back to the early 1900s and is often used as an insult.

这个用语要追溯到20世纪初。指的是周围拥有特定特征的人或者行为举止类似的人，便于区分出来。通常用于嘲笑或贬义，比方说，如果我说你是一个伪君子，然后你回复说，"我们彼此彼此。"

Make eyes at
向···抛媚眼

扫码看视频
Scan for video

Mary did not like the way Sally flirted with her boyfriend, the way she made eyes at him.

玛丽不喜欢莎莉和他男朋友调情的方式，不喜欢她向他抛媚眼的方式。

Teacher Josh Making eyes at someone indicates, through eye contact, that you find the person attractive and intend to get their attention. The phrase gained popularity in nineteenth century America.

这个用语在19世纪的美国广泛被使用。如果你对某人make eyes at，指的是你被对方吸引，希望引起对方的注意。

Pull yourself together

振作起来

扫码看视频
Scan for video

Pull yourself together man; stop shaking and start listening. We're in the middle of a war zone!

伙计，振作起来，不要再动摇，开始听好。我们在核心战斗区。

Teacher Josh This phrase means you should control your emotions and actions after being upset or agitated. While its origin is uncertain, its meaning is related to another idiom, "mind over matter," which appeared in Roman poet Virgil's *The Aeneid* in 70 B.C.

这个用语起源不是很确定。据所知，它的意思和另一个习语 mind over matter 很像。Mind over matter 是一个很老的习语，公元前 7 年，诗人维吉尔 (Virgil) 在他的诗中《埃涅阿斯纪》(The Aeneid) 使用。

It's not rocket science
很简单的事

扫码看视频
Scan for video

It's very easy, it's not rocket science. All you have to do is press the ON button.

这很简单，不是尖端科技。你所需要做的就是按一下这个打开按钮。

Teacher Josh This means something is easy to understand. The idiom, which gained popularity in the 1980s, compares an easy task or idea to rocket science, which is difficult for the average person without specific training to grasp.

在1950年，rocket science本来意思是火箭科学，泛指一些特别复杂的尖端科技，难度超出了一般人的能力。1980年之前，在美国习语中没有出现。现在多在否定句中使用，当说某事 not rocket science，指的是不复杂，很容易理解的事。

Cat nap
小睡

Johnny was tired so he took a cat nap, a quick rest while he was at work.

约翰尼太疲倦了，所以小睡了一会，即在工作的时候短暂休息片刻 。

扫码看视频
Scan for video

Teacher Josh

This describes a short period of sleep, usually taken in the daytime. The phrase, which originated in the early 1800s, was inspired by the short sleeps cats often take. A newer variation is "power nap."

Cat nap 指在白天短暂的小睡一会。19世纪初，人们已经开始使用该习语描述白天短暂的休息，就像猫咪白天经常打盹睡觉。还有一个类似的表达是 power nap，是日间小睡的意思。

Make or break
不成功，便成仁

Playing that role on Broadway will make or break his career. If he gets good reviews he'll be a star. If he doesn't, he'll always be an afterthought.

在百老汇扮演那个角色将会决定他事业成败。如果表演好，他就会成为一位明星。如果没有，以后没人会想到他。

扫码看视频
Scan for video

Teacher Josh

Make or break describes the factor which determines if someone or something will succeed or fail. Charles Dickens first used the phrase in *Barnaby Rudge*, published in 1840.

这个习语用来描述影响一个人或一件事成功与否的因素。比如说，圣诞节对小的零售商经营成败起关键作用。最早记载这个短语是查尔斯·狄更斯（Charles Dickens）在他1840年出版的作品《罗纳比·拉奇》（Barnaby Rudge）中使用。

Make matters worse
更糟糕的是

Not only did my pants get wet, but to make matters worse, my wallet was in my pocket.

不仅我的裤子湿了，更糟糕的是，我的钱包还在我的口袋里。

扫码看视频
Scan for video

Teacher Josh

This expression describes making an already bad situation worse. For example: "I was held up in traffic and missed my plane. To make matters worse, when I finally arrived at my destination, I fell and twisted my ankle."

这个用语的意思是使原本困难的，不好的情形变得更加糟糕。比方说，解释你为什么错过了航班，你可以说，我在来机场的路上交通堵车严重，当我到达机场的时候，我跌倒了并且扭伤了我的脚踝。更糟糕的是，我还忘了我的机票。

Know which way the wind is blowing
知道了现在的风向

We should try to know which way the wind is blowing before we put more money in the stock market.

在我们往股市投资更多钱之前，我们应该知道现在的风向。

Teacher Josh

Knowing which way the wind blows is to understand what is happening in situations that are not fixed, and to be able to accurately anticipate the future. This idiom was first used in the early nineteenth century.

19世纪初期，"the way the wind blows"已经使用，它的寓意是要明白在变化着的环境下知道会发生什么，并且有能力预期未来。

Wrap your head around something
认真考虑某事

扫码看视频
Scan for video

I'm trying to wrap my head around this equation,
to fully grasp it, but it's very confusing.

我试着认真考虑这个问题，争取全部理解，但是太令人困惑了。

Teacher Josh This means attempt to understand something that may be strange or out of the ordinary. The phrase has been in use since the 1970s.

这个用语指的是理解某事，特别指稀奇古怪和过时的事情。这个用语在美国东海岸已经流行了至少20多年了。有一个类似的表达 can't get my head around it，这个起源追溯到70年代，歌手Jim Croce用这个用语命名写了一首歌。

Down to earth
务实的；接地气的

扫码看视频
Scan for video

He's quite authentic, a very down-to-earth dude.

他是相当靠谱的；非常接地气。

Teacher Josh This phrase describes someone who is practical or reasonable, unpretentious and humble. It means someone the average person can understand well and relate to.

这个习语用来形容某人是务实的、通情达理的、不骄傲的、谦逊的。通常多指这个人很容易沟通，非常接地气。

Chew the fat
闲聊；闲扯

They're talkative, always chewing the fat together after class.

他们很善谈，经常下课后在一起闲聊。

扫码看视频
Scan for video

Teacher Josh To chew the fat means to talk with someone in a leisurely manner. It is believed that indigenous peoples in America chewed pork fat while casually chatting, and that British farmers did the same with smoked pork. Sailors were said to "chew the fat" to pass the time while out at sea.

Chew 的本义是"咀嚼"，那么，为什么咀嚼 fat 就是"闲聊"呢？这里的 fat 是什么？有一种说法说北美印第安人曾经坐在一起咀嚼猪肉干，一边咀嚼一边聊天，fat 指的就是 pork。在英国的农民也会坐在一起边咀嚼边聊天，水手也会这么做。所以 chew the fat 表示非正式的谈话或讨论，闲聊。

Test the waters
测试

扫码看视频
Scan for video

You'd better test the waters: first determine what your co-workers think before you submit that plan.

你最好在提交这份计划之前，测试一下你的同事在想什么。

Teacher Josh This may be derived from the preparation of a bath for a child; one would mix hot and cold water in a tub and dip a hand in to make sure the temperature is just right.

这个用语的来源可能和给宝宝洗澡有关。通常洗澡前，我们会将冷水和热水混合放在浴盆中，然后你把手伸到水里去测试水温，以确保水温不冷不热。

Pop the question
求婚

Aaron popped the question today. He asked me to marry him and gave me this ring.

艾伦今天求婚了。他请求我嫁给他，并且给了我这个戒指。

Teacher Josh This refers to a marriage proposal. When it first came to prominence in the 1700s, the question being asked could be about any other important issue.

这个用语在1700年已经被使用，意思是询问重要的问题，一般指求婚等重要的问题。到1820年，这个用语仅仅指求婚询问。

Brown nose
马屁精

Sally's classmates call her a brown nose because she gives their teacher an apple every day.

她的同学称呼莎莉为马屁精，因为她每天给她们的老师一个苹果。

扫码看视频
Scan for video

Teacher Josh

To brown nose means to try hard to please someone by being excessively attentive to them. For example: "She tried to brown nose her boss by spending a lot of time with him and giving him expensive gifts."

To brown nose意思是以一种很多人讨厌的方式努力取悦某人，以一种谄媚的方式奉承某人。举个例子，"She tried to brown nose her boss by spending a lot of time with him and giving him expensive gifts。"（她通过花费很多时间和他在一起，给他买昂贵的礼物，试图取悦她的老板。）

It ain't over 'til the fat lady sings
事情还没到最后

The team won the first three games of the series, but they need to win four to be the champions. It ain't over 'til the fat lady sings.

在这一季比赛中，这个队已经赢得了三场比赛，但是他们需要赢四场比赛才能成为冠军。事情还没有到最后，不能早下结论。

扫码看视频
Scan for video

Teacher Josh

This expression, which became popular in USA in the 1970s, means that one should not assume the outcome of a situation until it has ended as circumstances can change. It comes from the idea that an opera usually ends only after a talented singer (often stereotyped as fat) has delivered an amazing performance.

这个用语从1970年开始就比较流行，这是美国人的口头禅。指的是事情没有到最后，你不能假定结果，因为环境是变化的。这是歌剧用语，一些歌剧很长很无聊，但是在最后的时刻，如果有一名唱的好的歌手出现，她唱的很动听，最后会把一个无聊的歌剧变得精彩。
It ain't over 'til the fat lady sings中为什么说fat lady（胖的女士），通常情况下，唱的好的歌剧演员会微胖一些，所以用fat lady形容表演好的歌剧家。

Before you know it
很快；不知不觉中

I'm close. I will be there before you know it.

我已经很靠近。我很快就到达了。

扫码看视频
Scan for video

Teacher Josh This common expression means something that will occur sooner than one can imagine — in other words, very quickly. For example, one might think primary school students are a long way off from studying in college, but before you know it, they'll be preparing college applications.

Before you know it 是一个常用的短语，意思是很快，比你预想的要快。在进入大学之前，小学生会感觉还很遥远。但是时光飞逝，很快不知不觉，他们已经大学毕业了，迈向了人生新篇章。

It takes two to tango
一个巴掌拍不响

扫码看视频
Scan for video

Sarah tried to blame Kim for everything, but her teacher realized that they were both at fault. After all, it takes two to tango.

尽管萨拉将所有事都归咎于金姆，她的老师知道他们两个都有错误。毕竟，一个巴掌拍不响。

Teacher Josh This phrase, which is often used negatively, means that two people must be in disagreement for an argument to happen. The term implies that all parties involved should bear responsibility. It derives from the 1952 song, "It Takes Two to Tango."

这个用语起源于一首同名的歌曲，由Al Hoffman和Dick Manning演唱，在1952年发行。"It takes two to tango"中tango是双人探戈，跳探戈需要两个人同时跳，现多指一次争吵是两个人共同起作用的。在一次争论中，双方都要承担责任，多含有贬义。但是该用语也指：为了完成一个任务，必须要两个人同时参与。

Cannot bear the sight of

一见到···难受

扫码看视频
Scan for video

My mother-in-law is a mean and wicked old lady who always says nasty things. I cannot bear the sight of her.

我婆婆是一个刻薄的、邪恶的老女人，经常说一些难听的话。我一见到她就难受。

Teacher Josh If you cannot bear the sight of something, it means you do not want to be around it because of a strong dislike. Many people, for example, cannot bear the sight of blood. This can be used to refer to people as well.

Bear 指忍受，sight 指看见，"to bear the sight of"意思是接受或者忍受某人或某事，"cannot bear the sight of"意思相反，不能接受某人或某物，看不惯某人或某事，一见到就难受。比如说，"I cannot bear the sight of blood。It makes me faint。"（我一看到血就难受。血让我昏厥。）这个习语在日常生活中经常使用到。

Add insult to injury
雪上加霜

扫码看视频
Scan for video

Not only did he forget his homework, but to add insult to injury, he also forgot his teacher's name.

他不仅忘了做作业，雪上加霜，他忘记了他老师的名字。

Teacher Josh This phrase means to make a bad situation worse by giving more problems or hurting someone's feelings. It comes from "The Bald Man and the Fly," a tale in *Aesop's Fables*.

这个习语中insult是侮辱，injury是受伤，字面意思是在受伤的基础上再增加侮辱，指的是在已经很糟糕的的情形下，出现了更多的问题，增加了更多的羞辱与嘲笑。这是一个很古老的用语，来自伊索寓言"The Bald Man and the Fly"（光头与苍蝇）。

Easy come, easy go
来得容易，去得快

She never worried much about finances. For her, money was easy come, easy go.

她从来不担心财务问题。对于她，钱赚的快花的也快。

Teacher Josh This is used to describe something easily won and also easily lost. The origin of this informal phrase is unclear, though similar sayings have been around since the 1600s.

"Easy come, easy go"指来的容易去得快。这是一个非正式的用语。这个用语在美国已经使用了几十年，但是它的来源不清楚。这个习语曾经有以下表达"lightly come, lightly go", "quickly come, quickly go", 这几个从17世纪便开始使用了。19世纪之后演变成"easy come, easy go", 这个现在使用居多。

A snowball's chance in hell
毫无机会

His plan was so convoluted, there was only a snowball's chance in hell it would succeed.

他的计划太复杂了，要想胜利毫无机会。

Teacher Josh This is said about something that has little chance of succeeding. It refers to how a snowball would certainly melt in the extreme heat associated with hell. The expression was first used in 1880 in an article in the *Detroit Free Press*.

"A snowball's chance in hell"指的是做某事很难有机会成功。在1880年，这个用语最早在*Detroit Free Press*报纸发表的一篇文章使用，文章写道"Under the Hayes administration a Republican in the South has about as much chance as a snowball in hell. "Hayes是当时的美国总统，a Republican in the South 指美国南方的共和党候选人，has as much chance as a snowball in hell, 意思是南方候选人被当选可能很少。

Cat got your tongue
你怎么不说话了？

扫码看视频
Scan for video

Hey, why are you so tired? Cat got your tongue?

嘿，你为什么这么累？你怎么不说话了呢？

Teacher Josh
This question can be posed to someone who doesn't answer a question or has been remaining silent. It originates from the English Royal Navy, which used a cat-o'-nine-tails, a whip that has nine ends, to punish people. The person being flogged would be in so much pain that he would be unable to speak.

Cat got your tongue? 是一个问句。指某人问你问题，你却没有回答，保持沉默。这个习语的来源有两个解释：一个是英国海军曾经使用九尾鞭"cat-o'-nine-tails"鞭打犯人，鞭打后疼痛剧烈导致受伤者会很长时间保持安静；另一解释可能是来自古埃及，撒谎者和亵渎者的舌头要割下来喂猫，舌头没有了，自然不能说话。

Face the music
面对现实，承担后果

PRINCIPAL'S OFFICE

扫码看视频
Scan for video

He was caught cheating on the school test and now has to face the music.

他在学校考试中被抓住作弊，现在必须要承担相应后果。

Teacher Josh
To face the music is to accept the unpleasant results of one's actions. This American idiom dates to the 1830s, possibly having roots in the military where disgraced officers were dismissed to the beating of drums and band music.

这是一个美国习语，19世纪30年代在新英格兰地区流行。Face the music字面意思是面对音乐，实际上跟音乐没有关系，表达的意思是"承担后果"，这个后果不管是好是坏，都要接受。大多数情况都是不太好的结果。起源有两种说法：一种说法是来源于剧场，通常舞台前方有乐队为演员们伴奏，只要音乐一响，无论紧张与否，演员们就没有选择的余地，只能去face the music，因此这个短语就表示"面对现实"。另外一种说法来源于军队，犯了军纪的士兵接受惩罚去打鼓伴乐，后来用该短语指面对现实，承担后果。

No pain, no gain
没有付出就没有收获

扫码看视频
Scan for video

Sure, it's hard work; but no pain, no gain, right?
当然这是一项艰难的工作，但是没有付出就没有收获。

Teacher Josh This means that one will not improve without doing hard work, which might cause pain or discomfort. Actress Jane Fonda first popularized the phrase in her aerobics workout videos of the early 1980s.

这个习语流行始于 1982年之后，著名好莱坞女星 Jane Fonda（简方达）推广有氧运动健身操，她拍摄的十几部健身操风靡一时，在这些视频中，Fonda使用了"No pain, no gain"和"Feel the burn"短语作为健身理念的标语，健身初期会肌肉酸痛，过了这个阶段，便会达到燃烧脂肪的效果。所以现在 No pain, no gain 指的是没有付出就没有收获。

Left holding the bag
被迫留下收拾烂摊子

扫码看视频
Scan for video

Mary was forced to take responsibility for cleaning up after everyone else quickly left the party. She was left holding the bag.

所有人很快离开聚会，玛丽被迫承担打扫卫生的责任。她被迫留下收拾烂摊子。

Teacher Josh To be left holding the bag means one is put in an unfair situation, often taking responsibility for the actions of others. The phrase originated from Britain in the 1600s, and refers to a person having only an empty bag after all the valuable goods it contained had been removed by others.

Left holding the bag是比较久远的一个习语，最早使用于17世纪英国。起初的表达是"give one the bag to hold"，这个bag指的是空袋子。现在指让一个人为某事或某人承担责任和后果，通常是被迫接受。

An apple a day keeps the doctor away
一天一苹果，医生远离我

扫码看视频
Scan for video

He eats a lot of fruit every day to stay healthy. After all, an apple a day keeps the doctor away.

他每天吃很多水果，因为有益于健康。毕竟，一天一苹果可以远离医生。

Teacher Josh Popularized in 1913, this expression is based on a Welsh rhyme from the mid-1800s. It goes: "Eat an apple on going to bed and you'll keep the doctor from earning his bread."

"An apple a day keeps the doctor away"是1913年创造的，这个习语起源于英国的威尔士。149年前，在 Pembrokeshirc（彭布罗克郡）有一个谚语"Eat an apple on going to bed and you'll keep the doctor from earning his bread。"（上床前吃一个苹果，医生就无法赚钱了。）

When it rains it pours
祸不单行

扫码看视频
Scan for video

All four people in my house are sick right now. When it rains it pours.

我们房子里的所有四个人现在都生病了。真是祸不单行。

Teacher Josh This is a saying that came from an early 1900s advertising campaign for Morton Salt Company to promote its salt's free-flowing quality. It is now used to mean that when something good or bad happens, more similar things will follow shortly. The expression is usually used for negative events.

When it rains it pours，其中 rain 是下雨，pour 是涌出的意思，表面意思是当下雨的时候涌出来。这个习语的起源和 Morton Salt Company（莫顿盐业公司）有关，20世纪初，公司执行官创立了这个词，用来促销食盐，在天气不好的情况下，其他公司的盐容易粘在一起。公司想强调他们的盐即使在潮湿的天气下，也很容易从瓶子里倒出来，现在多指发生了坏的事情，而且坏事情在短期内发生了不止一次。

Buy a lemon
买假货

扫码看视频
Scan for video

Looks like Sal bought a lemon. I can't even get this car started.

萨尔看上去买了一个假货。这个车都不能启动。

Teacher Josh This refers to purchasing something worthless or not working well, usually a motor vehicle that has constant problems. The *Oxford English Dictionary* first listed this saying in print in 1909.

To buy a lemon可不是买一个柠檬，指的是买了一个没有价值的东西或者不好用的产品，特别指买了一个经常出现问题的交通工具。牛津英语词典显示这个习语最早出现是在1909年，使用起源于美国，lemon 这个词多指不满意的，劣质的，没有价值的东西。

Miss the boat
错失良机

We should have bought that house.
We missed the boat.

我们真应该买上那套房。我们错失良机了。

扫码看视频
Scan for video

Teacher Josh If you missed the boat, it means you did not take advantage of an opportunity when you could have. It can also mean you failed to understand something. This idiom is believed to have originated in Britain when ships were the main mode of international travel.

这个习语指的错过了一次良机。有时也指不能理解意思，比方说 "I missed the boat on that explanation"，指的就是我不能理解这个解释。这个习语曾经是一个书面语，起源于英国海洋俚语，严格来说，这个说法指因为到达太晚错过了航行，在以前，乘船是主要的交通

Pull someone's leg
逗别人；耍弄

When he told me he was royalty, I knew he was pulling my leg; there was no way it was true.

当他告诉我他是皇亲，我知道他在逗我，绝对不可能是真的。

扫码看视频
Scan for video

Teacher Josh This phrase, which has Scottish origins, means to make fun of others by deceiving them. It is possibly derived from a person tripping another over by pulling on his leg to make him stumble and look foolish.

这个习语起源于苏格兰，最早的意思是愚弄某人，多指欺骗他们。有一种说法是通过拉某人的腿使其绊倒，让对方看上去很傻。

Good things come to those who wait

好事情给那些等待的人

My college acceptance finally arrived. Mom was right that good things come to those who wait.

我的大学录取通知最后收到了。妈妈说的对，好事情给那些等待的人。

扫码看视频
Scan for video

Teacher Josh
This phrase means patience is a virtue. It originated in a poem, "Tout vient a qui sait attendre," by English writer Lady Mary Montgomerie Currie, who wrote under the pen name Violet Fane. The poem's title translates as "All hoped-for things will come to those who wait."

这个习语来源于一位诗人 Lady Mary Montgomerie Currie，20世纪初，她曾经用她的笔名 Violet Fane 写了一首诗，诗的名字是法文 "Tout vient a qui sait attendre"，翻译过来就是 "All things come to those who wait"，好的机会和事情是留给那些为之等待的人。

Get your goat

惹我生气

It really gets my goat when people talk during movies. I find it so annoying.

看电影如果有人聊天，真的会惹我生气。那样很令人讨厌。

扫码看视频
Scan for video

Teacher Josh
This means to irritate someone greatly, usually to the point of anger. American writer and critic H.L. Mencken attributed the phrase to the practice of putting a goat in the stall of a racehorse as a calming influence. Removing the goat from the stall of an opponent horse would make the horse nervous and agitated.

这个习语意思是惹怒某人，让某人生气。它的起源有争议，H.L. Mencken是一位美国的学者和记者，曾说过在比赛前，在盛放赛马的单间里放上一只羊，用来使马平静，但是在比赛开始前，把羊移走以使马紧张不安，但是此说法没有确切的证据证明。

Save for a rainy day
以备不时之需

扫码看视频
Scan for video

I put away a little money each week. I'm saving for a rainy day.

我每周都会存一点钱，以备不时之需。

Teacher Josh
This idiom means to keep something, usually money, until one really needs it unexpectedly in the future. The term comes from a practice farmers had of saving up money during better times, knowing that they might not earn much if poor weather affected their crops.

很多年以前，人们多数是靠天吃饭，特别是农民。由于在雨天是不能工作的，那么下雨就不能赚钱。农民努力提前存钱，他们知道在天气恶劣的时候没有收入。To save for a rainy day 指的就是存储一些物品，多指金钱，以备所需。

Take a powder
匆匆离开，逃跑

扫码看视频
Scan for video

He saw his mean uncle in the store so he took a powder, leaving as quickly as possible.

他看到他凶狠的叔叔在商店，所以他尽可能快的匆匆逃跑。

Teacher Josh In USA, a powder room is often an indirect or polite way to refer to the women's bathroom. If a woman excuses herself "to powder her nose," she is discreetly leaving to go to the toilet. However, these days it simply refers to leaving one place and going somewhere else, not necessarily to the bathroom.

在美语中，"powder room"是女士卫生间的一种委婉说法，"to powder one's nose"指的是一位女士需要立刻前往卫生间。因此，take a powder指的就是很快的判定要离开，不需要过多的评论。

Drink like a fish

过度饮酒，酒量大

That guy has a serious drinking problem — he drinks like a fish.

那个人酗酒，喝很多酒。

Teacher Josh

This idiom describes a person who drinks a lot of alcohol. It originated in *The Night Walker, or The Little Thief*, a play by John Fletcher and James Shirley that was published in 1640. It refers to how a fish appears to drink a lot as it lives in water and opens its mouth often.

这个习语起源于1640年，Fletcher 和 Shirley 在文学作品中 "The Night Walker or the Little Thief" 使用。Drink like a fish 从字面看是像鱼一样喝水，因为鱼本身生活在海洋中，周围都是水，鱼会喝很多水，但是如果像鱼一样喝酒，指的就是喝酒喝多了。

Down the hatch

喝完它

扫码看视频
Scan for video

I disliked the taste of the cough medicine, so I swallowed it in one gulp, right down the hatch.

我不想吃咳嗽药，所以我一口吞下去喝完了。

Teacher Josh

This describes swallowing a portion of liquid, often alcohol, all at once. It derives from the idea of a ship's hatch, through which cargo and people would pass to enter. The hatch — a small doorway — is similar in function to one's mouth.

Down the hatch，其中 hatch 是指船的甲板上的大舱口，用来把货物送下货舱。这个习语很可能来自水手，他们看惯了把大批货物从舱口下到货舱里，于是拿这样的运作来比喻自己的一种生活嗜好，那就是把酒一饮而尽。这个形象生动的比拟从20世纪三十年代开始流行至今。

The bottom line
最重要的一点；最终结论

扫码看视频
Scan for video

If she says no to my prom invitation, the bottom line is that she just doesn't like me.

如果她拒绝我的毕业舞会邀请，最重要的原因是她不喜欢我。

Teacher Josh This phrase originated in the USA during the 1960s to describe the last line of a profit and loss statement, where a final calculated number is indicated. It would show the total profit or loss made by a company. This expression now refers to the most important element or point of a situation. For example: "The bottom line is, men don't change very much after marriage."

"The bottom line"是一个地道美国式的短语，最早由一位公司职员于20世纪60年代创立，用于描述财务盈亏表的结果，表中有最终的数据，用以判断一个公司最终是盈利还是亏损。现在这个习语指一件事中非常重要的考虑。比方说"The bottom line is, men don't change very much after marriage。"这句话意思是"男人最重要的一点是他们婚后不会改变。"此句中bottom line不是底线的意思，而指的是最重要的一点，最明显的一点，无可辩驳。

Get off your high horse
别自以为是

She thinks she's so much better than everyone else, but I told her to get off her high horse.

她以为她比其他人要好很多，但是我告诉她别自以为是。

扫码看视频
Scan for video

Teacher Josh This is used to tell someone to stop being arrogant. A rider on a large horse would be physically above others, which is why those with military or political power in the past would ride on large horses, making a show of themselves being powerful and superior by being above the crowds. To be on a high horse came to metaphorically mean someone being proud.

To get off your high horse 这个习语从字面意思来看，是从你的高高的马上下来，实际意思是停止扮演优胜者；停止自大与傲慢。这个习语指的是大的马，特别是军马。那些有军权或政权的人常常会选择最大的马去骑，以显示他们的权利。因为骑在马上的高度可以让他们在人群中高一些，但这不代表他们一定高人一筹。所以人们现在多使用隐喻意思，指"别自以为是，别傲慢"。

A hot potato
棘手的问题

扫码看视频
Scan for video

I wouldn't discuss that in the office, it's too controversial
– a real hot potato.

我不会在办公室讨论这个问题的，太有争议，一个棘手的问题。

Teacher Josh This phrase describes something controversial or a situation awkward to discuss. It originated in the mid-1800s and is used often in writing about politics. A reporter, for example, may write that a politician is unlikely to speak on a controversial subject as it is "a political hot potato."

这个习语起源于19世纪，多指一个争议的事件或情况，处理起来很棘手，不愉快。换句话说，就是一个没人想要处理的难题。这个习语在政治活动中经常被提及。比如，记者想访问候选人，会问很多问题，包括一些让候选人不舒服的棘手问题，这些问题称为"political hot potato"，因为问题有争议。

Every cloud has a silver lining

守得云开见月明

扫码看视频
Scan for video

He struck out, but his mom told him that every cloud has a silver lining — something good will come out of it.

他出局了，但是他的妈妈告诉他守得云开见月明，好事情迟早会有的。

Teacher Josh This means in every difficult situation, there is a positive aspect to be found, so one should not feel hopeless, as things will become better. The phrase originated in the John Milton's poem, *Comus* (1634).

Every cloud has a silver lining 来源于John Milton's（约翰弥尔顿）于1634年写的诗歌代表作《Comus》。这个习语不是说云里有闪亮的衬衫里子，而是说黑暗中总有一丝光明，永远不要放弃希望，因为祸兮福之所倚。苦难就像乌云cloud遮住了阳光，银色的衬里silver lining意味着终会冲破乌云，再次让一切变得光明。如果你有一个同事工作心力交瘁，你可以说，"I know you feel stressed, but don't worry, things will get better soon. Every cloud has a silver lining。"（我知道你压力很大，但是不要担心，事情很快会变好。守得云开见月明。）所以，熬过困难就会有拨云见日的一天。

Bent out of shape
十分生气

Ken got all bent out of shape when his dinner fell off the table. He was inappropriately angry.

当他的晚餐从餐桌上掉下来，肯恩十分生气。他不同寻常的生气。

扫码看视频
Scan for video

Teacher Josh When someone gets bent out of shape, they are angry or upset. This idiom became popular in the mid-1900s and is thought to originate from scuba diving. If a diver gets decompression sickness, also known as "the bends," he will most likely experience pain in his joints, such as the elbows and knees. He will no doubt feel "bent out of shape" or upset.

To get bent out of shape 意思是生气和失望。这个习语流行于20世纪初，在日常讲话中使用。有人推测起源于可怕的潜水病，水肺潜水会随着潜水深度增加，对耳朵造成一定压力，很痛苦，the bends指的就是潜水病。Get bent out of shape 的 bent 听起来很像 bends。潜水病患者肯定不开心，反而很沮丧得了病，患者都精神和身体都 bent out of shape 了。简单来说，"get bent out of shape"就是生气的同义词。

Throw shade
影射

扫码看视频
Scan for video

Jerry insulted Mary; he threw shade on her by hinting that she's not attractive.

杰里侮辱了玛丽，他影射出她很丑。

Teacher Josh To throw shade at someone is to make a comment that indirectly shows disapproval or insults them. If you say to a friend, "Look at your haircut!" the person could interpret this to mean the haircut looks silly.

Throw shade最早源自同性恋的社群文化，后来才被广泛使用，意为用细微、非语言方式在公众场合蔑视某人。当某人巧妙的侮辱另一个人，这个习语是合适的。比方说，你不喜欢你朋友的发型，你可以说"看看你的发型！"这些单词本身没有侮辱的意思，但是通过说话的语气朋友可能会理解为发型很糟糕。这就是一种微妙的侮辱。

Add fuel to the fire
火上浇油

扫码看视频
Scan for video

He lied to his mom about where he spent the night —
and then he added fuel to the fire by telling a second
lie: he said he hadn't been drinking when in fact he
had been out with friends at a beer party.

关于他晚上去哪里了，他对他妈妈撒谎；紧接着，他火上浇油
地撒了第二个谎：他说他没有喝酒，然而事实上他和朋友们在
酒吧喝酒了。

Teacher Josh

When you add fuel to a fire, you are
making a miserable situation worse. If one
pours fuel on a fire, the fire gets bigger.
This expression has existed in Latin since 1 A.D.

在公元一世纪，这个习语存在于拉丁文中，
罗马历史学家提图斯·李维（Titus Livius）在他
的著作《罗马自建城以来的历史》用到。Add
fuel to the fire现在多指，因为你说了或者做了
某事，让糟糕的情况变得更糟。众所周知，当
你往火上撒油，火会越烧越旺，更加危险。因
此，这是一个比喻的说法。如果一位妻子因为
老公没有赚很多钱而生气并且凶他，同时还因
为其他的事情责怪他，这无疑是火上浇油。

Shape up or ship out
要么改进，要么离开

Peter's boss gave him an ultimatum on his work performance — he was to shape up or ship out.

他的老板给皮特下了最后通牒：要么改进工作，要么被解雇。不改进就离开。

扫码看视频
Scan for video

Teacher Josh This means if one does not improve in behaviour or mindset, one should leave. The phrase originated in the US military during World War II. It was said to those who were not behaving as soldiers should, as a warning to be better or else be sent out to fight overseas. It has since been used in other situations — asking someone to improve in their performance or risk being asked to leave.

这个习语来源于二战时期美国军队，从字面意思来看，要么成为一名士兵，水手和海军，要么被送到海外战争地区。前面to shape up 的意思是改进你的工作或行为，后面一半 to ship out 就是运送你离开一个地方。把前后两部份合在一起 to shape up or ship out 就成了一个俗语，意思是：要么改进工作，要么离开。美国的陆军里经常用这个习语，战争结束后，可以用在任何想提高成绩的场景。比如说，经常老板警告员工，要么改进工作，要么解雇你。

Red carpet treatment
贵宾待遇

When our soccer team returned home after winning the championship they received the red carpet treatment with a parade in their honor.

当我们的足球队赢得冠军后回到家乡，他们满载荣誉游行，被给予贵宾的待遇。

扫码看视频
Scan for video

Teacher Josh This refers to a special way of handling someone, usually accorded to royalty. The idiom originated in the twentieth century and comes from the practice of rolling out a carpet for an important guest to walk on.

Red carpet treatment 指的就是特殊待遇，一般指皇家接待所使用的待遇。一般在接见重要人物时，接待单位总是铺上红地毯以表隆重和热烈，所以这种"红地毯待遇"就表示"贵宾待遇"了。尽管铺红地毯很久前就出现，但是这个习语是在20世纪才流行起来的。

You can lead a horse to water but you can't make him drink

你可以给他人提供帮助，但是你无法强迫他接受

He was told not to walk on that ice, and yesterday he fell through! You can lead a horse to water, but you can't make him drink.

他被告知不要在冰上走，可是昨天他却穿越冰层掉下去了。你可以给别人提供帮助，但是别人不一定接受。

Teacher Josh This expression, dating back to the twelfth century, means that you can try your best to help someone by providing him with opportunities, but you can't compel him to make use of those opportunities.

这句话直接翻译过来的意思是"你可以把一匹马牵到河边，但是你不能强迫它喝水。"实际上是一个比喻："你可以给别人提供一些帮助、机会或者其他东西来使事情变得简单，但是你没法强迫他去做。"这个比喻的说法可以追溯到12世纪，1546年在John Heywood's 谚语集中曾出现。

Through thick and thin

同甘共苦

I love this man and I'm staying with him no matter what, through thick and thin.

我爱这个男人，无论发生什么，我都会和他在一起，同甘共苦。

Teacher Josh This means to continue supporting someone through difficult times. This phrase dates from the 1300s and refers to a forest, where some areas are thick in vegetation, while some are sparse. If someone accompanies you on a journey through a forest, he passes through thick and thin with you.

这个习语可以追溯到14世纪，英国当时还不是现在大家看到的这番繁荣面貌，而是像小乡村一样，有很多树林，有浓密的(thick)和稀疏的 (thin)。人们穿过浓密的比较困难，而穿过稀疏的会容易很多。因此用这个短语来比喻生活的困难和快乐，从而引申出"同甘共苦、有福同享有难同当、不离不弃"等类似的意思。简单来说，强调无论任何情况下，都会在一起。

Sick as a dog
病的非常严重

扫码看视频
Scan for video

I feel sick as a dog, I'd better take my blood pressure.

我感觉病的非常严重，我最好量一下我的血压。

Teacher Josh If one feels as sick as a dog it means one is not feeling well. In some cultures, dogs were viewed as dirty and diseased animals. This phrase was first used in literature in 1705.

习语"sick as a dog"首次书面使用是在1705年，当形容一个人病的很重时，英语中有这样的说法"sick as a dog"。为什么人们会用"狗"来表示"生病"的意思呢？因为狗很贪吃，而且经常乱吃东西，当吃下去的食物导致身体不适时，狗会呕吐并且反应激烈，因此人们就用sick as a dog来描述病得很严重的样子。

Fortune favors the bold

幸运眷顾勇敢者

扫码看视频
Scan for video

It was bold of him to set his speaking fee at $10,000, but the lecture was a sellout. Fortune favors the bold!

他大胆定价演讲费为一万美金，演讲票竟然售空，幸运眷顾勇敢者。

Teacher Josh This means luck is on the side of risk-takers. The old saying, which derives from the Latin proverb "*audentes Fortuna iuvat*," is used as a motto by many American military units.

这是一个很老的谚语，起源于拉丁谚语 "*audentes Fortuna iuvat*"，意思是幸运往往眷顾那些敢于冒险的、大胆的人。曾经是几所美国海军舰船和美国空军飞机的座右铭。

All mouth and no trousers
光说不做

扫码看视频
Scan for video

He acts like he's a ladies man, but when it comes to actually asking a woman for a date, he gets nervous. He's all mouth and no trousers.

他看上去很有女人缘，但是当真的和一位女士约会的时候，他就紧张。他光说不做。

Teacher Josh This saying, which gained popularity in England in the 1970s, describes someone who talks boastfully but does not have any intention or ability to carry out his claims.

All mouth and no trousers从字面看指"全是嘴，但没裤子"。很奇怪，这是什么意思呢？如果一个人整天叨叨，那确实是 all mouth 浑身是嘴，如果 no trousers没穿裤子，哪位能出去干活呢？所以光说（all mouth）不做（no trousers）就是光说不练，和汉语"光说不做假把式"同义。

Cover all the bases
面面俱到

扫码看视频
Scan for video

Before the first man walked on the moon, scientists covered all their bases, preparing for any possible mishap, by testing rockets and making sure all equipment worked flawlessly.

首位宇航员在月球上行走之前，科学家们通过测试火箭，面面俱到准备着任何可能的事故，通过测试火箭确保所有的设备运行完美。

Teacher Josh This means to prepare everything carefully in advance to ensure things go smoothly. In preparing for an English language exam, one might say: "I think I've covered all the bases — I studied grammar and vocabulary, practiced reading and writing, and memorized 300 idioms."

当你说cover all the bases，意思是为了确保事情进展顺利，你会提前认真地检查和准备。在准备一项英文测试，一个人会说"I think I've covered all the bases — I studied grammar, vocabulary, practiced reading and writing, and memorized 300 idioms。"（我认为我已经面面俱到，我学习了语法、词汇，练习了阅读和写作，并且记住了300个习语。）

Eyeball to eyeball
面对面

I need a one-on-one meeting with Fred. I want to talk to him eyeball to eyeball.

我需要和弗雷德开面对面会议。我想和他面对面交谈。

Teacher Josh If you are eyeball to eyeball with someone, you are meeting them face to face or in direct contact with them. It is used to imply conflict or hostility — eyeball to eyeball meetings often involve both parties staring angrily at each other. This saying was first recorded in the 1960s.

这个习语最早记录在20世纪60年代。如果你和敌人或某人争吵，眼珠子睁大直接盯着对方，就是 eyeball 对着 eyeball，现在指面对面。通常 eyeball-to-eyeball meeting 是敌对的会议，举个例子，"They had an eyeball-to-eyeball confrontation。"（他们是对峙的。）

Well begun is half done
好的开端是成功的一半

Once you've memorized your lines for the first two acts of the play, you can easily memorize the rest. Well begun is half done.

你已经记住了这个剧本的头两段表演的台词，所以你可以轻松地记住剩下的。好的开端是成功的一半。

Teacher Josh This means that if you handle the early tasks in a project properly, it is easier to do the remaining tasks or complete the project. Greek philosopher Aristotle used the expression in his work.

这是一个比较老的谚语，亚里士多德曾经使用它。意思是指一个项目开始做的好，后面做起来就更容易。

Cut somebody some slack
放某人一马

扫码看视频
Scan for video

He was learning to drive so he asked the policeman to cut him some slack and not give him a ticket.

他正在学习开车所以他请求警察饶了他，放他一马，不要开罚单。

Teacher Josh When someone cuts you some slack, they are giving you more time or another chance to do something, or being less strict with the rules. The saying derives from the nautical world in the mid-1900s, describing a slackening of tautness in a rope or sail. A similar expression is "give someone a break."

这个习语起源于二十世纪中叶，cut切，slack指绳索的富余部分，cut someone some slack通过给某人切一段绳子，使得原先的绳子变得更长、更松弛，slack就是松弛的意思。如果你是工作中的新人，工作中犯了错误，同事和老板会因为你是新人而原谅你犯的小错误，降低对你的要求 (give you some slack) 。所以 "To cut someone some slack" 意思是给某人更多的时间或者机会去做某事，另一个常见的同义词是give someone a break （饶了某人）。

Get something out of your system
发泄；代谢

扫码看视频
Scan for video

I'm still dizzy from that cough syrup. I'll feel better when I get it out of my system.

那个糖浆令我头晕目眩。当糖浆从我身体里代谢出去，我就会感觉好多了。

Teacher Josh This saying has three meanings. The first is to expel something from the body. The second is to no longer be preoccupied with a nagging desire. For example: "I got partying out of my system during college. I'm ready for a quieter life." The third is to release pent up anger.

这个习语实际上有三个意思。首先，字面意思是"从你的身体代谢出某物"。举例，"You'll feel better once you get whatever caused the food poisoning out of your system。"（把导致你食物中毒的东西代谢出去，你会感觉好一些。）第二个意思是"不再做一些不想做的事情"。举例，"I got partying out of my system during college. I'm ready for a quieter life now。"（大学期间喝酒聚会，我现在不想做了。我想过安静的生活。）第三个意思是"发泄"，把藏在心中许久或忍耐很长一段时间的事情说出来，释放一下。

Look before you leap
三思而行

Since you can't decide whether to marry Jack, my advice is to date other guys first. Look before you leap!

既然你不能决定是否嫁给杰克，我的建议是先和其他男孩约会，三思而行。

Teacher Josh This phrase means one should not act without considering the consequences. It comes from *Aesop's Fables*, in a tale about a fox who was unable to climb out of a well and convinced a goat to leap into the well. The fox then climbed out on the goat's horns and left the goat trapped in the well.

这个习语意思是一个人不应该在没有认真考虑结果前行动。在伊索寓言中有一个故事讲到，一个狐狸掉到井里爬不上来，然后狐狸劝山羊跳到井里帮助他。然后狐狸爬到山羊的犄角上从井里跳出来，山羊却被困在井里了。这个故事映射出一个道理，就是Look before you leap，做事三思而后行。

Ignorance is bliss
无知是福

扫码看视频
Scan for video

She thinks her husband is taking the kids to McDonald's, but in reality he is taking them to a sports bar to watch the game. Ignorance is bliss.

她以为她丈夫带孩子们去了麦当劳，但他实际上带他们去了酒吧看比赛。无知是福。

Teacher Josh This idiom means if you do not know about something, you will not worry over it. Originating in the eighteenth century, it is derived from a poem, "Ode On a Distant Prospect of Eton College" written by Thomas Gray.

18世纪，英国诗人 Thomas Gray在文章 "On a Distant Prospect of Eton College" 中写道 "Where ignorance is bliss, / 'Tis folly to be wise'"。这个习语指如果你不知道某事，你就不用担心。还有一个类似的表达 "What you don't know doesn't hurt。"

Shake a leg
快点

Hurry, shake a leg or you'll miss the train.

快点跑，快点，否则你会错过火车的。

扫码看视频
Scan for video

Teacher Josh This is used to tell someone to move more quickly. It may have originated during the American Civil War, when those carrying the wounded off the battlefield would shake an injured soldier's leg or arm to check if he were alive or dead.

Shake a leg 可不是摇晃腿的意思。这个习语的起源有点模糊，但是有人称来自美国内战。每次战争结束后，担架兵便会去田地里找寻受害者，通常会快速地摇晃士兵的腿和胳膊，以便得出结论：士兵活着还是已经死亡。现在我们说shake a leg，意思是你想让某人快点行动，快点走。

Once bitten, twice shy
一朝被蛇咬，十年怕井绳

扫码看视频
Scan for video

I've learned my lesson about how important it is to carry an umbrella. The day it rained I had none with me. I got soaked! Once bitten, twice shy.

携带一把伞是非常重要的，我已经得到教训。有一天下雨了，我什么也没拿，我被淋得湿透了！真是一朝被蛇咬，十年怕井绳。

Teacher Josh This phrase is used to indicate that someone will not do something a second time because they had a bad experience doing it the first time. If you fall in love and that someone rejects you (once bitten) you may be reluctant to fall in love again (twice shy). The idiom dates to the nineteenth century.

Once bitten, twice shy 这个习语可追溯到19世纪，指的是一个人一旦第一次做事有不好的经历，那么第二次就不会做了。如果你爱上一个人，这个人拒绝了你。Once bitten 受伤了，第二次就不会让自己再爱了。

Make a mountain out of a molehill
小题大做

扫码看视频
Scan for video

You got a B and you're acting like you failed. You're making a mountain out of a molehill.

你得了一个B，但是表现的像没及格。你有点小题大做。

Teacher Josh This idiom, which has been around since the sixteenth century, means to react as though a small problem is really serious. It compares the size of small heaps of soil made by moles burrowing in the ground (molehills) to that of mountains.

这个习语16世纪才出现。鼹鼠是小的掘洞哺乳动物。他们在土中挖洞，挖出的土堆到地面上，从而形成一个小山丘，这个山丘叫做 molehill。因此，make a mountain out of a molehill 指的是把小的事情搞大，小题大做。

Get a kick out of it (something)
使人感到非常愉快

扫码看视频
Scan for video

I'm a terrible dancer, but I still enjoy it — I still get a kick out of it.

我跳的不好，但是我很享受，跳舞使我很愉快。

Teacher Josh   This means to get enjoyment or excitement from something. For example: "I get a kick out of watching the children play" means I really enjoy watching them play. This idiom comes from "I Get a Kick Out of You," a song written in the 1930s.

这个习语来源于20世纪30年代的一首歌，歌的名字是"I Get a Kick Out of You"。Kick就是用脚踢的意思，但是，这首歌的名字"I Get A Kick Out of You"却毫无痛苦之意，相反的，它的意思是：由于你的爱情使我感到快乐和激动。现在用来描述任何一位使你高兴的人，或任何一样令你喜爱和激动的东西。举个例子，如果你看到一个小孩弹钢琴很好，你可以说"I get a real kick out of seeing her play so well at such a young age。"

Don't put all your eggs in one basket
不要孤注一掷

扫码看视频
Scan for video

It's best to invest in a variety of stocks, not just one. Don't put all your eggs in one basket.

最好投资多只股票，而不是一个。不要孤注一掷 。

Teacher Josh This idiom is advice to not depend on one thing by placing all of one's hopes and focusing one's efforts on it, in case one loses everything at once. It was used in the novel *Don Quixote* by Miguel de Cervantes and it became popular in the seventeenth century.

这个习语在17世纪流行起来，出现在米格尔·德·塞万提斯的著作《唐·吉诃德》中。意思是不要把所有的资源都放在一个地方，不要把你的钱、希望和未来压在一件事上。众所周知，鸡蛋很易破，如果你把所有的鸡蛋都放在一个容器（basket）内，一旦这个容器损坏，你将会瞬间失去所有的鸡蛋，很难过。

Bark up the wrong tree
用错精力

扫码看视频
Scan for video

If you think I'm loaning you money again, you are asking the wrong person. You're barking up the wrong tree.

如果你认为我会再次贷款给你，你找错人了，用错精力了。

Teacher Josh This means to take a course of action — usually making a request — that fails because of mistaken thinking. The expression, which has been popular since the 1820s, comes from the idea of a dog barking mistakenly at a tree that it thinks its prey is on.

Bark up the wrong tree字面意思是对着错误的树吼叫。传说与打猎有关，狗因为嗅觉的灵敏和身手的敏捷而被用来追踪猎物。狗在看到猎物时，就很有可能去追。逃跑的猎物就会上树，于是狗就会在树下叫。但有时候狗会犯错误，就是没有找到猎物藏身的那棵树，那么这个时候够就 bark up the wrong tree了。这个习语自19世纪20年代流行起来，现多指找错目标，用错精力。

Don't give up your day job
做好眼下的工作（让某人不要追求不可能成功的事情）

He was so bad at hanging wallpaper that his wife facetiously told him, "Don't give up your day job."

他贴墙纸很糟糕，所以他的妻子开玩笑地对他说："做好眼下的工作。"

扫码看视频
Scan for video

Teacher Josh This is a humorous way of advising someone not to pursue something he is not skilled at. For example, if someone is a terrible singer, a friend may tell him not to give up his day job, implying that he should not switch careers to become a singer as he would not earn money being one.

Don't give up your day job 中的 day job 是指你的日常工作，依靠它可以赚薪水。这个习语是用一种幽默的方式建议某人不要追求不可能成功的事情。如果我唱歌很糟糕，我问朋友是否喜欢我的歌，她会开玩笑地说"Don't give up your day job。"（做好眼下的工作。）如果我唱歌很糟糕，那么放弃现在的工作去寻找一份职业歌手的工作就是冒险。

Skate on thin ice
冒险做事

扫码看视频
Scan for video

Georgette is skating on thin ice if she thinks her mom won't find out that she sneaks in and out of the house through her window.

乔吉特正在冒险：她未经许偷偷爬窗户出去，她以为她妈妈不会发现。

Teacher Josh To skate on thin ice means to do something risky or be in a dangerous situation. This idiom alludes to the danger of walking on thin ice, as there is a high possibility of the ice breaking. It was first used figuratively by American writer Ralph Waldo Emerson in his essay, "Prudence" (1841): "In skating over thin ice, our safety is in our speed."

Skate on thin ice 意思是冒险做一些危险的事情，可能会导致坏的结果。这个习语指在薄薄的冰面上滑雪，却冒着冰面破裂的危险。最早是美国作家和哲学家拉尔夫·沃尔多·爱默生在他的文章中引用，1841年他在论文Prudence中这样写，"In skating over thin ice, our safety is in our speed。"（在薄冰上滑雪，我们的安全取决于我们的速度。）

G.O.A.T.
最棒的

扫码看视频
Scan for video

Millions of fans think Michael Jordan is G.O.A.T. — the greatest of all time.

数百万粉丝认为迈克尔·乔丹是最棒的。

Teacher Josh This acronym stands for the "Greatest Of All Time" and is usually used to describe people who are exceptional in their fields, particularly athletes and musicians. Famed boxer Muhammad Ali was popularly known as "The Greatest." This later became "G.O.A.T." or the greatest of all time.

G.O.A.T.是Greatest Of All Time的首字母缩写，意思是赞扬非同一般的运动员、音乐家和其他公共人物。这个表达来源于美国著名拳击手—穆罕默德·阿里，他有一个昵称叫"The Greatest"。后来演变为"the Greatest Of All Time"，多指最伟大的，世界上没有任何人可以与之相媲美。

A picture is worth a thousand words
百闻不如一见

扫码看视频
Scan for video

The editor told the author to add photographs to his text because a picture is worth a thousand words.

编辑告诉作者多添加照片到文本，因为百闻不如一见。

Teacher Josh This idiom means that it is easier to convey something using a picture than to describe it in words. It came from the Chinese philosopher Confucius and was popularized in the West in the early twentieth century.

这个习语在20世纪早期美国西部流行，但最早来源于孔子——中国一位伟大的哲学家。
A picture is worth a thousand words意思是一幅图胜过千言万语，图片比起文字更有说服力，百闻不如一见。

Sweet tooth
喜好甜食

扫码看视频
Scan for video

With his sweet tooth, he would never be able to resist having that cake.

由于喜欢甜食，她绝对抵挡不住蛋糕的诱惑。

Teacher Josh Dating to the 1300s, this idiom describes a craving for sweet foods, such as candy, baked goods and ice cream, among others.

Sweet tooth 起源于14世纪，指的是非常喜欢甜的食物，比如蛋糕和冰激凌。如果说你有 sweet tooth，意思是你非常享受并沉溺于这些美味的食物中。

Kill two birds with one stone
一举两得

For me, riding a bike to the post office kills two birds with one stone. I save on the taxi fare and get to drop off my tax forms.

对于我而言，骑着自行车去邮局是一举两得。我不仅省下了出租车车费，同时还送交了纳税文件给政府。

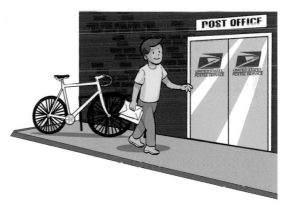

扫码看视频
Scan for video

Teacher Josh This idiom means to achieve two different aims in a single action. Its origin is unclear but one theory is that it comes from the Greek myth of Daedalus and Icarus, who escaped from Crete using wings made of bird feathers. Daedalus is said to have obtained the feathers by killing two birds with a single stone.

习语的起源不是很明确，但是有一种说法是说来自Daedalus and Icarus（代达罗斯和伊卡洛斯）。Daedalus是希腊有名的建筑师，Icarus 是他的儿子，希腊神话中说他们被囚禁于克里特岛上。为了逃走，Daedalus用一个石头打下两只鸟，并用鸟的羽毛做成了翅膀，然后飞离小岛。Kill two birds with one stone 现在多指做一个活动，可以同时完成两个目标，解决两个问题。

Burn the midnight oil
熬夜

扫码看视频
Scan for video

I'm going to have to study hard all night. I will have to burn the midnight oil to pass tomorrow's geography test.

我整晚不得不努力学习。为了通过明天的地理考试，我不得不熬夜。

Teacher Josh This means to stay awake until really late in the night to work or study. It originates from a time when light was provided by oil lamps or candles. This expression was first used in a seventeenth-century poem by Francis Quarles.

Burn the midnight oil起源可追溯到17世纪的一位英国诗人Francis Quarles（法兰西斯·夸尔斯），在古代，人们通过点燃煤油灯或蜡烛代替现代的灯，所以习语中出现burn燃烧、midnight半夜、oil油。Burn the midnight oil 就是深夜还在学习或工作，也就是熬夜。

On the ball

机警，靠谱

扫码看视频
Scan for video

Billy cleaned the kitchen spotlessly in no time. He's really on the ball.

比利马上把厨房打扫得一尘不染。他很靠谱。

Teacher Josh This idiom describes someone who can quickly understand something and do it well. The phrase comes from sports — probably baseball as it implies that by keeping your eye on the ball you will likely get a hit and get on base safely.

这个习语的来源和运动有关，有可能是棒球。通常说"keep your eye on the ball"，意思是紧盯着球，然后击中得分胜利。On the ball 可不是在球上的意思，而是指一个人很机警和机灵，从而很快的理解某事，他们在自己从事工作的领域做的很好。

Beat a dead horse

白费力气

You've told me that it is raining over and over again. You're beating a dead horse. I know it's raining: I'm soaked!

你已经对我说了很多遍正下雨。你是仕白费力气。我知道正在下雨，我全身已经湿透了。

扫码看视频
Scan for video

Teacher Josh To beat a dead horse is to waste effort on a situation that cannot be changed. For example, if you continue talking about a matter that has concluded, you are beating a dead horse. This expression dates to the nineteenth century and comes from the practice of striking horses with a riding crop (whip) to make them run faster. Beating a dead horse does not achieve anything as a dead horse will not run at all.

这个习语起源在19世纪中期，通常用鞭子beat a horse，可以让马跑的更快，但是如果鞭策一匹死马就毫无意义了，哪里也去不了。Beat a dead horse现多指在某件事上白费力气，之前讨论过的一个问题再继续讨论也是白费力气。

Compare apples to oranges
根本不同的事情

扫码看视频
Scan for video

Being an excellent violinist has nothing to do with having big muscles. You are comparing apples to oranges.

成为优秀的小提琴家和有发达的肌肉没有关系。你在比较根本不同的事。

Teacher Josh
This first appeared in a collection of proverbs by John Ray and is used to mean two dissimilar items are being compared with each other. The qualities of an apple can be compared with those of another apple because they are both the same fruit. However, comparing an apple with an orange is silly since they have completely different characteristics.

这个习语早期出现在17世纪70年代John Ray的谚语集中，用来描述对比完全不相关的两个物品或两件事。你可以对比这一批苹果和另外一批苹果，但是如果对比苹果和橘子就没有意义了。Compare apples to oranges 现在多指完全不同的事。

At each other's throats
唇枪舌剑争吵

扫码看视频
Scan for video

Kenny and Betty argued every single day. They were at each other's throats.

肯尼和贝蒂每天都争吵。他们唇枪舌剑的争吵。

Teacher Josh
This means two people are arguing angrily with each other. It is usually used to describe serious conflicts, not mild disagreements.

At each other's throat 字面意思是抓住对方的喉咙，想要把对方勒死，实际上应用于争论中，而不是通过身体物理斗争。现在是指严重的争吵，而不是温和的争论。

Take the wind out of your sails
使某人泄气

扫码看视频
Scan for video

When I found out I didn't get the promotion, it took the wind out of my sails — I felt depressed.
当我发现我没有被提升，真让人泄气，我很失望。

Teacher Josh

This means to dash someone's aspirations, or make them less confident or hopeful by doing something unexpected. The term comes from sailing, as sailing a ship against the direction of the wind removes the advantage of using wind energy to help power a ship forward.

To take the wind out of one's sails 意思是使某人失去信心和希望。一艘船迎风航行很难，阻力重重，现在多比喻保持自信和乐观向上的能量在减少。

Slap on the wrist
轻微的处罚

Giving that rich guy a $20 fine is no punishment at all
— it's like a slap on the wrist.

处罚那个有钱人二十美金的罚款，和没处罚一样，处罚太轻了。

Teacher Josh

This idiom, which means a light or weak punishment, originated in eighteenth-century England. A literal slap on the wrist was given as a form of mild punishment.

Slap on the wrist 这个习语中，slap是给耳光，wrist是腕部，在腕部上扇一下，形容处罚很轻微。这个习语可能起源于18世纪英国，那个时代处罚通常很严重，所以slap on the wrist指轻微的处罚。

Busy as a bee
像蜜蜂一样忙碌

Can we meet tomorrow instead? I'm very busy, as busy as a bee today.

我们能不能明天见面？我太忙了，像蜜蜂一样忙碌。

Teacher Josh

This expression, which means having a great number of things to do, is used in *The Canterbury Tales*, a collection of stories written in the fourteenth century. It likely comes from the observation of bees flying from plant to plant and working hard to collect nectar.

这个习语起源于十四世纪，出自乔叟(Chaucer)的《坎特伯雷的传说》(Canterbury Tales)。众所周知，蜜蜂是田间勤劳的昆虫，嗡嗡穿梭于植物间。所以说某人busy as a bee意思是说像蜜蜂一样忙碌。

Feeling blue
心情不好；无精打采

Jack is sad that his girlfriend left him. He feels blue.

杰克因他女朋友离他而去伤心。他心情不好。

Teacher Josh

If you are feeling blue you are feeling very sad. Sadness has been linked with the colour blue for a long time. In the 1800s, "to go blue" meant that one is in the final moments of one's life and will pass away shortly.

Blue 是蓝色，蓝色一般和悲伤有关联。在19世纪，如果说go blue，多指一个人的医疗状况已经到达生命的最后一个阶段，所以feel blue 指的是感觉伤心难过，很忧郁。

Jump on the bandwagon
跟风；随大流

扫码看视频
Scan for video

It's annoying when fans jump on the bandwagon and root for the Yankees only when they are winning.

粉丝们跟风坚信洋基队会胜利，真是令人讨厌。

Teacher Josh This means to take part in or support an activity that is recently well-received by others or successful. This phrase was first used in America in 1848, when a famous clown used his bandwagon drawn by horses to transport politicians around town to give campaign speeches. When this became successful, more and more politicians wanted to be on the bandwagon.

Wagon 的意思常指四轮马车，bandwagon 可指"浪潮，时尚"。Jump on the bandwagon 指"跟风，随大流"，用来支持一个流行的活动。习语源于十九世纪的美国，当时马戏团每到一个城市，都会组织热闹非凡的游行队伍来吸引当地的观众。第一次是在1848年使用，一位有名的小丑使用他的马戏团四轮马车运送政客，车上的音乐吸引公众到达竞聘演讲的地方。

Calm before the storm
暴风雨前的平静

Bill's Cafe is empty now, but believe me — it's the calm before the storm. By noon it'll be packed!

比利的咖啡馆现在是空的，但是相信我，这仅仅是暴风雨前的平静。到中午就会满员。

扫码看视频
Scan for video

Teacher Josh This refers to a time that is quiet or without any activity, just before a time with a great amount of activity or trouble. It likely comes from weather observations. Sometimes, before a storm breaks, there is a period of stillness, when dark clouds are overhead but no wind or rain.

这个习语几百年前曾被使用，起源和一种天气现象有关，通常在暴风雨来袭之前有一段平静的时期。Calm before the storm现在指在强烈的活动到来前，有一段时间是没有活动或少活动。

A snowball effect
雪球效应

扫码看视频
Scan for video

The combination of the howling wind, the pitch-black night and being alone has a snowball effect of making you feel scared.

咆哮的狂风，漆黑的夜晚与孤独的结合会产生雪球效应，会使你越来越害怕。

Teacher Josh A snowball effect describes a situation in which something grows bigger with increasing speed. It comes from the idea of a snowball rolling down a snowy hill. As the snowball rolls, it collects more snow and grows bigger, which makes it roll down the hill even faster.

这个习语描述的是滚雪球的场景，想象雪球从一个山坡上滚下来，刚开始是一个小球，在向下滚的过程中会卷起更多雪，然后这个雪球就会越来越大，同时重力也会越来越大。现在多用来描述一种情形，事物大小或重要性以越来越快的速度增长。通常这个雪球效应产生的结果是消极的，但是也不全是。比如举个例子："Studying two vocabulary words every day will have a snowball effect: before you know it you'll have mastered thousands of words。"意思是指每天学习两个单词也会产生雪球效应，不知不觉你便会掌握上千个单词。

Birds of a feather flock together

物以类聚

扫码看视频
Scan for video

We dress so alike that when people see us they say birds of a feather flock together.

我们穿的很像，人们常常说我们物以类聚。

Teacher Josh Originating in the sixteenth century, this expression means that people with the same interests or similar personalities get along well and can be found together. It refers to how birds of the same species fly together and congregate in the same places.

Feather在这里不是一片羽毛，而指的是同一类羽毛。拥有同类羽毛的鸟是不是经常聚在一起呢？是的。我们经常会看到鸽子和其他鸽子聚在一起，乌鸦和其他乌鸦聚在一起，很少看到乌鸦和鸽子聚在一起。这个习语自16世纪开始使用，指的是拥有相同品味和兴趣的人们，意译为物以类聚，人以群分。

A far cry from
与···大相径庭

Living in Miami is a far cry from living in Siberia. It's very different.

生活在迈阿密与生活在西伯利亚大相径庭。非常不一样。

Teacher Josh

This expression means that two or more things are very different. It evolved from its literal meaning of two places being such a long distance apart that if a person in one place were to cry out, another person in the second place would not be able to hear him.

Be a far cry from something 指的是事物之间非常不同。这个习语是从字面意思延伸过来的。A far cry 原先指一段距离，距离太远以致于不能轻松的呼叫。如果有一个人大喊，另一个人很难听到，因为他们离的太远了。

Cut a rug
热情地跳舞

Wow! Does she cut a rug! She's a great dancer.

哇！她在热情地跳舞！她是一位伟大的舞蹈家。

Teacher Josh

This expression dates to the 1920s and means to dance enthusiastically or really well. In some movie portrayals of house parties, guests would roll up the host's rug before dancing because energetic dancing could tear a rug or wear it out.

这个表达起源于20世纪20年代。在早期电影中，我们会看到青少年去别人家跳舞前会卷起一个小地毯。精力充沛的跳舞很快会使毯子磨损。所以"cut a rug"指满腔热情地跳舞，我们也可以说"cut some rug"。

A dime a dozen

很普通；不值钱

There are thousands of movie scripts; they are a dime a dozen.

成千上万本电影剧本随处可见，这些很普通，不值钱。

扫码看视频
Scan for video

Teacher Josh This refers to something that is common and possibly worthless. A dime is a ten-cent coin in the USA and Canada. In the past, many everyday goods, such as eggs and apples, were sold at a dozen (twelve) for a dime. As they were plentiful, they had low value and were sold cheaply.

Dime 是美元中的10分，相当于汉语中的"一角钱"。Dime 第一次使用是在1796年，在19世纪的美国，一些商品的广告中经常使用a dime a dozen，比如鸡蛋和苹果等物品。Dozen指的是一打十二个，所以当我们说"a dime a dozen"，指的是某物很常见，不值钱。

Weather the storm

渡过难关

Our marriage was in terrible shape, but we forgave each other, weathered the storm and are now doing well.

我们的婚姻曾经很糟糕，但是我们彼此原谅，共渡难关，现在相处很好。

扫码看视频
Scan for video

Teacher Josh To weather a storm is to persevere and successfully handle serious problems. This expression, which has been used figuratively since the seventeenth century, has a literal meaning as well. It means to wait where you are until the bad weather passes.

To weather the storm 字面来看是风暴来临，待在原地不动直到暴风雨结束，和紧急疏散相反。自1650年之后，该习语多使用比喻的表达，意思是尽管遭遇严重困难，依然可以继续前行。

Chicken out
临阵退缩

扫码看视频
Scan for video

Yeah, I chickened out. I decided to get out of there because I didn't want to get myself killed.

是的，我临阵退缩。我决定逃离那里，因为我不想自杀。

Teacher Josh If you "chicken out," you decide against doing something because you are afraid. It originated in the seventeenth century when its early use was in the context of calling someone a coward.

To chicken out 起源于17世纪，用来形容一个人胆小，因为胆小决定不做某事。William Kemp是一名英国演员，他曾经在《Nine Days' Wonder》《9天的奇迹》中使用这个习语形容某人是懦夫，胆小鬼。后来，查尔斯·狄更斯等作家在文学作品中也使用。

Blow off steam
发泄

扫码看视频
Scan for video

The best way to blow off steam, to get rid of tension,
is to dance enthusiastically.

发泄不满、释放压力的最好方式是疯狂的跳舞。

Teacher Josh This means to release strong emotions by doing something that helps one relax or is enjoyable. The phrase comes from the nineteenth century, when steam engines were newly developed, with no way of removing steam pressure automatically. To avoid an explosion, the steam would have to be manually released to be "blown off."

这个习语来自于早期的铁路建设，那时火车没有安全阀门。当蒸汽（steam）压力上升，工程员便会通过释放（blow off）蒸汽来降低压力，从而防止爆炸。To blow off steam 意思是通过参加愉快的、剧烈的、放松的活动，以此来释放不好的情绪或能量。这个习语在19世纪中期普遍使用。

Let someone off the hook
让某人免于责罚

扫码看视频
Scan for video

Bill hurt my feelings by saying I'm terrible at tennis, but I forgave him. I let him off the hook, and we're still good friends.

比尔说我打网球很差伤害了我，但是我原谅他了。我让他免于责罚，我们还是好朋友。

Teacher Josh This means to let someone escape from trouble or responsibility. A fish will be in serious trouble if it gets caught on a hook, but if the fisherman lets it off the hook, it will escape trouble. In the example, Bill is let off the hook by the person he insulted. That person decided not to confront Bill for hurting him.

Hook 是鱼钩，off the hook 就是一条鱼摆脱钓鱼者的鱼钩，同理，指脱离困境，免于责任。在上面的例子中，被比尔侮辱的人决定放下问题，不去讨论，放弃权利，不去与诽谤他的人进行对抗，我们就说"Let Bill off the hook。"

Champ at the bit
迫不及待

扫码看视频
Scan for video

Eileen couldn't wait until Macy's opened. She was champing at the bit to buy new shoes.

艾琳等不及梅西百货开门。她迫不及待地想买新鞋子。

Teacher Josh If you champ at the bit you are eager to do something. The phrase was originally used to describe horses that chewed on their "bit" or mouthpiece when they were excited.

To champ指咀嚼，bit指马要咬的东西，马龙头的一部分，如果马多次咬这个bit，是因为马有点躁动。所以 champ at the bit 指迫不及待的着手做某事。这个比喻的用法开始于19世纪中期。

117

You can't make an omelette without breaking eggs

有失才有得

I don't like putting a road through beautiful country, but you can't make an omelette without breaking eggs.

我不喜欢穿越美丽的国家而建设道路，但是有失才有得。

扫码看视频
Scan for video

Teacher Josh

This means to make or achieve something great, there will be sacrifices. It traces its origins to a French soldier and politician, François de Charette. When asked about the deaths of many soldiers in war, Charette used this expression in his response.

习语来源于18世纪法国，François de Charett 是一位法国的士兵和政客，1796年他将法语翻译为英语。Omelette是早餐中的鸡蛋饼，如果不打碎（break）几个鸡蛋，怎能做好鸡蛋饼呢？Make an omelette without breaking a few eggs表达的意思是为了完成某事，牺牲是必要的。

Go back to the drawing board

从头再来

扫码看视频
Scan for video

We must go back to the beginning, back to the drawing board, and figure out how to properly put up a fence.

我们必须回到开始，从头再来，找出怎样专业的搭建一个篱笆。

Teacher Josh

This means going back to the earliest stages of planning to make changes after an unsuccessful attempt at something. The phrase originated in a cartoon caption that appeared in the *New Yorker* magazine in 1941.

这个习语起源于二次世界大战时《纽约客》杂志上的一幅漫画。在漫画中，很多军人奔向一架坠毁的飞机，而设计这架飞机的工程师把图纸夹在胳膊底下，默默地走开了。漫画的标题是："Go back to the drawing board。"意思是从头再来，再设计一架。现在多指做某事的过程中遭遇失败，于是从头再来。

As right as rain

身体健康；令人满意

扫码看视频
Scan for video

Going home always feels so comfortable —
as right as rain.

回家总是让人感觉很舒服，令人满意。

Teacher Josh Originating in nineteenth-century England, this is used to describe being in good health, particularly after being slightly ill or hurt. This phrase can also refer to something working as it should.

As right as rain 指的是身体健康，一切顺利。这个习语起源于19世纪英国，一般用来描述某人身体很健康。如果一个人生病了或者手术之后，他们感觉很健康，我们可以说 "someone is right as rain。" 在上面的例子中，"as right as rain" 指的是回家的感觉特别棒，令人满意。

On top of the world
非常幸福

扫码看视频
Scan for video

With her new car and new job, Rachel felt like she was on top of the world.

新车和新工作，瑞秋感觉非常幸福。

Teacher Josh If you feel on top of the world, it means you feel very happy. This phrase became popular in the early twentieth century.

这个习语始自20世纪，被很多作家在作品中使用。如果你感觉"on top of the world"，意思是你非常开心，非常幸福。

Between a rock and a hard place
进退两难

Faced with confronting the mob or jumping off the cliff, the thief was between a rock and a hard place.

要么面对民众，要么跳下悬崖，这个小偷陷入进退两难处境。

扫码看视频
Scan for video

Teacher Josh This idiom describes a situation in which one has no good options. It comes from the Greek mythology of Charybdis, a large and powerful whirlpool; and Scylla, a man-eating, cliff-dwelling monster. The two are threats to sailors and also located close to each other. Saying one is stuck between a rock (the cliff) and a hard place (the whirlpool) has been a way to describe being caught in a dilemma.

这个习语指进退两难，起源于古希腊神话。据荷马史诗记载，Odysseus（奥德修斯）要经过卡律布迪斯（Charybdis）一个奸诈的女巫和漩涡；Scylla 吃人的住在悬崖（cliff）边上的怪物。一边是女巫（a hard place），一边是悬崖怪物（a rock），此时面临的是进退两难处境。所以 这就是 between a rock and a hard place的来源。

Teach an old dog new tricks
很难让人们接受新事物

扫码看视频
Scan for video

I gave my recipe for meatballs to my grandmother but she refused to try it. You can't teach an old dog new tricks.

我给奶奶我做肉丸子的食谱，但是她拒绝尝试。很难让她接受新事物。

Teacher Josh This describes the difficulty of helping someone learn something new or change their habits. It originated in the sixteenth century and appeared in John Heywood's 1546 collection of proverbs.

这个习语是英国作家 Heywood 于1546年发明的，被认为是传统英语中最老的习语之一。意思是很难去教顽固的人一些新鲜事物，因为他们固定用他们的思维方式，并且不愿意去接受不同。

Without shadow of a doubt
无可置疑地

Given the evidence against the man, the jury found him guilty without shadow of a doubt.

有了针对这位男士的证据，法官无可置疑地认定他是有罪的。

扫码看视频
Scan for video

Teacher Josh: This describes being certain that something is true. The phrase originated in eighteenth-century England. "Beyond a shadow of a doubt" is a similar expression.

这个习语起源于18世纪的英国，常用来表达我们对某事很确定，无可置疑。举个例子，Teacher Josh's students, without a shadow of a doubt, will improve their English if they study idioms。（Josh 老师的学生，如果好好学习习语，毫无疑问会提高他们的英语水平。）

All thumbs
笨手笨脚

Suzy was not good at knitting. She was all thumbs.

苏西不擅长编织。她笨手笨脚。

扫码看视频
Scan for video

Teacher Josh: This describes someone being very clumsy or awkward with their hands. For example: "Harry tried to fix the chair, but he was all thumbs." This means Harry struggled to fix the chair as he was bad at handling the chair parts and tools. This phrase dates to the 1500s.

这个习语起源于16世纪，all thumbs 实际是"your fingers are all thumbs"的简写。从字面意思翻译是"你的十个手指全是大拇指"，因为大拇指又短又小，所以不灵活，现在多指形容一个人笨手笨脚。举个例子，"Harry tried to fix the chair, but he was all thumbs。"（哈利想去修理这个椅子，可是他笨手笨脚。）

Eyes in the back of one's head
眼光敏锐

扫码看视频
Scan for video

Mom must have eyes in the back of her head because she always knows when I'm about to misbehave.

妈妈第六感敏锐，因为当我一旦要行为不端，她总是知道的。

Teacher Josh This phrase describes someone who is keenly observant, who knows what is going on even when she cannot see it. The expression first appeared in *Aulularia*, a play by Roman playwright Plautus. It was also cited by Dutch philosopher Erasmus in his collection of proverbs.

Eyes in the back of one's head 从字面意思来看，是脑袋后面长着眼睛，实际意思是形容一个人拥有不同寻常的观察力，眼光敏锐。习语起源于罗马时代，在普劳图斯（Plautus）的著名喜剧《一坛黄金》（*Aulularia*）中出现，作家伊拉斯谟在他的格言集中曾引用。

123

Snowed under
忙得不可开交

I've been overwhelmed with work — snowed under all weekend.

我被这些工作压倒了，忙得不可开交。

Teacher Josh This phrase describes having such a great deal of work to do that you feel as if you are being suffocated. It was first used in an 1880 newspaper article describing how a blizzard had covered everything in snow.

Snow 是雪，snowed under 被雪压在下面，这个短语第一次被使用是在1880年，在一篇新闻中描述一次暴风雪把一切都覆盖在雪下。To be snowed under 意思是指有很多工作要去做，这些工作多的让人快窒息了，不言而喻，就是忙得不可开交。

Under the table
幕后交易

The boxer was accused of accepting money under the table to purposely lose the fight.

拳击手被控告秘密接受贿赂，幕后金钱交易，从而故意输掉比斗。

Teacher Josh This idiom, popular since the 1950s, is used to describe a secret and illegal exchange of money. For example, "All the workers were paid under the table to avoid taxes."

Under the table 字面意思是在桌子下面，实际上指的是非法幕后交易，多用来形容使用金钱完成非法交易。这个习语自20世纪中期便被使用，举例，"All the workers were paid under the table to avoid taxes。"（所有的工人为了避免交税，都是幕后交易支付工资。）

Throw caution to the wind
不顾一切

He threw caution to the wind and jumped off a cliff to complete his first bungee jump!

他不顾一切地跳下悬崖，完成了他的第一次蹦极跳。

Teacher Josh This idiom, which originated hundreds of years ago (some say it's from John Milton's *Paradise Lost*; others believe it's from a fourteenth-century prayer), is used to describe risky behavior without regard for the consequences.

这个用语起源于几百年以前，通常用来描述进行有风险的行为，不考虑其后果。有些人认为来自英国诗人弥尔顿的《失乐园》，其他人认为来自一篇14世纪的祷文。

Waste not, want not

勤俭节约，吃穿不缺

扫码看视频
Scan for video

Betty planned the family meals so that everything she purchased from the supermarket on Monday was consumed by Friday — waste not, want not.

贝蒂为家庭用餐做好计划，每次周一去超市买的东西周五都会消耗掉，真是勤俭节约，吃穿不缺。

Teacher Josh

This adage means that if one does not waste anything, one will always have enough. The phrase was coined by English writer Maria Edgeworth in her book, *The Parent's Assistant* (1796).

Waste not, want not 指的是如果你不浪费，你就永远拥有，什么也不缺。这个谚语是英国作家玛丽亚·埃奇沃思（Maria Edgeworth）于1800年在书籍《The Parent's Assistant》中使用，到19世纪已经被人们广泛使用，但是当代在一次性文化氛围中很少听到了。

You can say that again

完全赞同

扫码看视频
Scan for video

Jimmy said that the geography test was very difficult. Billy thought so too, as he responded with, "You can say that again."

吉米说地理考试太难了。比利同意，表示完全赞同。

Teacher Josh

When you want to show that you completely agree with something that was just said, you can reply, "You can say that again." This informal saying gained popularity in the first half of the 1900s.

You can say that again 字面意思看是让你把话再说一遍，然而，这个习语可不是让你把话重新说一遍，而是表达自己非常赞同对方的观点。这个习语起源于20世纪上半叶。举个例子，一位美国学生也许会对另一位说，"Chinese is difficult. I can't pronounce even basic words."（汉语太难学了。我连基本词都不会发音。）另一位学生会说"You can say that again！"，表示完全赞同。

Cold turkey
突然戒掉某习惯

扫码看视频
Scan for video

He has quit drinking soft drinks. He has gone cold turkey because he has just started on a diet, and a can of soft drink has 160 calories!

他突然完全停止喝汽水。他突然戒掉这个习惯，因为他刚开始节食，而每罐汽水有160卡路里。

Teacher Josh To go cold turkey means to suddenly stop doing something, usually to quit a bad habit. When a drug addict goes cold turkey, she is trying to quit her addiction abruptly. This expression alludes to the appearance of a drug addict going through withdrawal — much like a cold turkey that's pale and clammy.

Cold 寒冷，turkey 火鸡，cold turkey 是寒冷的火鸡吗？通常 cold turkey 前面会接 go 这个动词，指一下子就突然戒掉瘾或坏习惯。一种说法是因为冷火鸡肉可以立即食用，不需要特别加热处理，所以用它来形容立即戒掉某事。另一种说法是，这个词最早用来指戒毒瘾的人，戒毒初期他们可能经历全身发冷和起鸡皮疙瘩的症状，正如同一只冰冻的无毛火鸡。日常生活中，只要下定决心即刻戒掉任何一种习惯，cold turkey 都可使用。

Off one's rocker

行为反常；发疯的

扫码看视频
Scan for video

Meredith must be off her rocker if she thinks she can swim across the English Channel without any training.

梅雷迪斯肯定是神经病，如果她认为她不需要培训，就可以游泳穿越英吉利海峡，她发疯了。

Teacher Josh This expression is used to describe someone who is acting in a bizarre way. Originating in the 1800s, it likely alludes to someone who has fallen off his rocking chair — the result of having acted in a strange manner.

这个习语起源于19世纪末期，关于习语中为什么包含rocker没有明确的说明，可能和rocking chair有关。从摇椅上掉下来，也很荒唐可笑的。现在说某人off their rocker，意思是这个人行为反常，发疯了，愚蠢可笑。

Chalk it up to
把 · · · 归因于

When Billy failed his math test, his teacher told him to chalk it up to not studying.

当比利数学测试没有通过，他的老师告诉他失败归因于没有学习。

扫码看视频
Scan for video

Teacher Josh This connects a particular reason to explain the result of something. For example: "Low voter turnout was chalked up to a dull campaign." This means that the reason for fewer people voting was because many people were not interested in the campaign. In contrast, to "chalk up" means to score points or achieve success in a game. For example: "Our baseball team chalked up another victory."

To chalk it up 意思是把某事发生归于某特殊原因。比如，"Low voter turnout was chalked up to a dull campaign。"（少量选民出席归因于无趣的竞选。）为什么没有很多选民参与，是因为竞选效果不大。注意习语去掉 it 变成chalk up，意思是在比赛中得分或取得胜利。可以说，"Our baseball team chalked up another victory。"（我们的棒球队再次取得胜利。）

A leopard can't change its spots
本性难移

扫码看视频
Scan for video

Her dad just can't stop being mean; it's who he is. A leopard can't change its spots.

她的爸爸粗鲁易发脾气，他就是那样的人。本性难移。

Teacher Josh This means that it is not possible for someone to change their character. It usually describes a person with a negative trait, such as a tendency to lie or an addiction to stealing. The idiom is derived from ancient Greece and appears in the Bible.

A leopard can't change its spots 起源于古希腊语，在圣经中出现。字面意思是"一只豹子不能改变它的斑点"，比喻一个人无论多么努力改变，也很难改变自己的个性。通常用来形容某人的弱点很难改变，比如形容一个人连环撒谎或者偷盗成瘾。

Put something on ice
把···搁置起来

He dreamed about being the mayor of New York City, but when he reached his seventieth birthday, he decided to put it on ice and enjoy retirement for a while.

他梦想着成为纽约市长，但当他过70岁生日时，他决定把梦想搁置起来，然后去享受退休生活。

扫码看视频
Scan for video

Teacher Josh Literally, chilling food or beverages on ice helps to stop them from going bad for a period of time. Thus, this figurative expression describes holding off on doing something until some time in the future. It is usually used to talk about delaying an action, such as a business plan.

Put something on ice 从字面意思来看是"把…冷藏（食物、饮料）"。喻指推迟做某事，通常是一份行动计划，一份商业计划书。我们可以说一份商业计划因为经济衰退暂时被搁置了。

Cut corners
走捷径

If you cut corners while painting by applying only one coat, you'll surely need to redo the job next year.

如果你在刷墙的时候走捷径，只刷一层，你明年肯定会再做这个工作的。

扫码看视频
Scan for video

Teacher Josh To cut corners is to use the easiest, cheapest or quickest way to do something, often resulting in a less than ideal outcome. When encountering a sharp turn, if a driver goes diagonally across a corner instead of following the road, he is said to have cut a corner. It may shorten the journey but it endangers lives.

To cut corners 意思是用最简单的，最便宜的，最快速的方式做事。当你开车经过一个直角拐弯，你没有开车径直到头拐弯，而是急拐弯对角线穿过去，这就叫做"cut the corner off"。虽然这样会节省时间，但是有撞上路牙石和侧翻的风险。所以"cut the corner off"指的是放弃正常的安全路线，抄近路，快速到达终点。

Best of both worlds
两全其美

扫码看视频
Scan for video

He was a champion swimmer and an honors student.
He was popular among his peers and got recognition
from his teachers — he had the best of both worlds.

他既是游泳冠军，又是荣誉学生。真是两全其美。

Teacher Josh Someone who has the best of both worlds is in a situation of having the benefits of two different things. For example, some people believe that a person who did good deeds on earth will enjoy the fruits of his good deeds in heaven, thus getting the best of both worlds.

圣经中描述一个人活着的时候做了好事，去世后到了天堂可以获得收获，所以一个人做了好事，可以享有两个世界的美好。Best of both worlds 习语来源于此，在20世纪中期流行使用。现在指做某事会两全其美。

Have your head in a cloud
富于幻想，脱离实际

扫码看视频
Scan for video

If he doesn't understand how dangerous it is to ride a scooter without wearing a helmet, he must have his head in a cloud.

如果他不明白骑电动车不带头盔的危险性，他肯定是脱离实际了。

Teacher Josh This phrase means that one is so unaware of what is going on around him that he dreams of doing what is impractical or impossible. For example, someone who is poor at math and wants to become a mathematician has his head in a cloud.

Have your head in a cloud 其字面意思是"把脑袋伸到云彩里"，喻指想法飘飘然，富于幻想而脱离实际，也指不聪明。如果一个人数学很糟糕，却还想成为数学家，我们可以说这个人"has his head in a cloud"，这个人不现实，富于幻想。

Anybody's guess

难以预料

Nobody can accurately predict who will be the next president. It's anybody's guess.

没有人能准确预测谁会是下一任总统。真是难以预料。

扫码看视频
Scan for video

Teacher Josh When something is anybody's guess, it means no one can be certain about what is really true or likely to happen. For example: "Nobody can predict when the stock market will rebound; it's anybody's guess." This saying originated in the thirteenth century.

这个习语起源于13世纪，anybody是任何人，anybody's guess 意思是谁也说不准，任何人都不确定。没有人可以预测股市什么时候回升，这里我们就可以说股市回升 "is anybody's guess"，股市难以预料。

In hot water

遇到麻烦

扫码看视频
Scan for video

Whoever took Tom's basketball is in hot water. Tom is going to beat him or her up.

无论是谁拿走了汤姆的篮球，他都会遇到大麻烦，因为汤姆决定要殴打他。

Teacher Josh You don't want to be in hot water, as it means you are in trouble. This saying originated in the early 1500s and is used in everyday speech.

这个习语是起源于16世纪早期，现在在日常口语中广泛使用。In hot water，字面意思是在热水里。想象一下你掉到热水里，肯定不舒服，遭遇大麻烦。所以现在用 hot water 指遇到麻烦，或与某人在一起很尴尬。

Make off with (something)
偷走；拿走

He made off with my bag. He just grabbed it right out of my hand and ran away.

他偷走了我的包。他从我手里夺走包并且逃走了。

扫码看视频
Scan for video

Teacher Josh This means to run away with something that has been stolen. It's an informal way to say that someone took something that does not belong to them. For example: "They broke in and made off with my computer."

"To make off with"意思是偷走某物，然后逃走，这是比较好听的说法。举个例子，"They broke in and made off with my computer。"意思是他们入室偷走了我的电脑。

Let sleeping dogs lie
别惹麻烦

扫码看视频
Scan for video

Please don't discuss that bumpy plane ride we had last month; it will bring back bad memories. Let's not talk about it any more; let sleeping dogs lie.

请不要再讨论上个月颠簸的飞机旅行，想起来都是噩梦。我们还是不要再讨论了，别惹麻烦。

Teacher Josh This is advice to leave a bad but inactive situation alone, as interfering might stir up trouble. If you see a pack of sleeping dogs, would you wake them up and risk having them biting you? Better to let sleeping dogs lie. This phrase has been around since the 1300s.

Let sleeping dogs lie 字面意思是"让正在睡觉的狗躺着"。如果你看见一群狗在睡觉，你会冒着被咬的风险去叫醒它们吗？我想不会的，最好让它们在那里躺着。这个习语在14世纪出现的，现在多指不要盲目干预，以免招惹麻烦。

Cut the mustard
符合要求

扫码看视频
Scan for video

I didn't cut the mustard as a table tennis player —
I could never win a match.

我不符合作为一名乒乓球选手的要求，我永远不会赢得一场
比赛。

Teacher Josh

If you cut the mustard, it means you are able to succeed or meet expectations. However, "doesn't cut the mustard" is more common, meaning someone doesn't meet expectations or something is inadequate. This is an idiom that dates to the late 1800s.

这个习语来源于19世纪的美国，cut是切，mustard是芥末，直译"切芥末"显然不通，这里指不能成功或者满足期望。通常与don't /doesn't 连用，形容某事不符合要求或某人不能胜任工作。

Stir (up) a hornet's nest
捅马蜂窝

扫码看视频
Scan for video

The teacher said something that was controversial, stirring up a hornet's nest.

这位教师说了某些事然后引起争议，在学生那里捅马蜂窝了。

Teacher Josh This idiom, which dates to the 1700s, describes causing trouble. Think of what would happen if you poked a hornet's nest. Undoubtedly, the hornets would be unhappy and angry!

这个习语起源于18世纪早期。Hornet是黄蜂、胡蜂或者马蜂。 Stir up a hornet's nest相当于中文的俗话"捅了马蜂窝"。如果一个人捅马蜂窝，会怎么样？ 马蜂肯定不会开心的，这个人必然会遭到大群马蜂的叮刺围攻，这就是自找麻烦。

That ship has sailed
为时已晚

扫码看视频
Scan for video

We used to be good friends but we've been through too much to be close again. That ship has sailed.

我们曾经是好朋友，但是我们经历了太多不可能亲密无间了。一切为时已晚。

Teacher Josh This idiom means the opportunity to do something has passed and is no longer possible. It comes from the idea of someone who is running late to board a ship. Once the ship has departed from the harbour, the person would have missed his chance to be on that voyage.

这个习语指错过机会，一切不可能了。想象你要乘坐一艘船，但是你来晚了。你到了港口却发现船已经离开了。你不能乘坐这艘船了。你错过这次机会了，没有人会帮你再次乘船。一切为时已晚。

A perfect storm
面临重重危机；祸不单行

She was fired from her job on the same day that her cat died. It was the perfect storm — two terrible things happened at the same time.

她被公司解雇了，同一天，她的猫咪去世了。真是祸不单行，同时发生了两件糟糕的事情。

扫码看视频
Scan for video

Teacher Josh A perfect storm refers to a terrible situation that results from a combination of many things happening around the same time. The idiom is popularized by Sebastian Junger's book, *The Perfect Storm* (1997), which documents a fishing vessel crew encountering a cyclone known as the Halloween Gale.

Perfect 除了完美，还可以表示极致的，极端的。A perfect storm 指极端的天气。这个习语来自塞巴斯蒂安·荣尔（Sebastian Junger）的一本散文书《完美风暴》，书中讲述了一艘渔船在海上遇上了好几次暴风雨。A perfect storm 除了形容天气，多指同时遭遇多件不好的事情，祸不单行。

Last straw
促成一件事发生的最后一推

When he slapped her, she left him immediately. It was the last straw.

他扇了她一耳光，她便立刻离开他。那是最后的一根稻草。

扫码看视频
Scan for video

Teacher Josh This idiom comes from an Arabic saying about loading a camel beyond its capacity to move. At a certain point, a single straw of grass will overwhelm the desert-roaming beast, causing it to collapse.

这个习语从字面意思指压垮骆驼脊背的最后一根稻草。习语来源于阿拉伯语，往骆驼身上增加负荷，超过了骆驼的承受能力，有时候，再多加一根稻草，骆驼便会倒塌。现多指促成一件事情（多指不好的事情）发生的最后一推，尽管事情本身或许微不足道，但是却让持续已久的问题最后爆发。

Icing on the cake
锦上添花

The tickets for the show were a wonderful gift, but the fancy dinner afterwards was the icing on the cake.

演出的门票是一个极好的礼物，然而随后精致的晚餐更是锦上添花。

扫码看视频
Scan for video

Teacher Josh This describes having a wonderful finale to something that is already good — a memorable day, for example — so that it becomes even better. Icing is a delicious sugary coating used to decorate a cake. While the cake itself looks and tastes delicious on its own, the icing improves it.

Icing on the cake，意思是在蛋糕上面加上糖衣（icing），这项发明创立于17世纪。试想，一个美味的蛋糕即使从中间尝一口也会很好吃，但是如果品尝最上面带糖衣的部分，那肯定是最好吃的。这个糖衣让原本比较好吃的蛋糕变得完美。如果我们描述某事是"icing on the cake"，意思是锦上添花，让好的事情变得更好，但这件事并不是必需品。

Pushing up daisies
死亡

Henry will be pushing up daisies soon if he continues to skydive. His parachute may not open one day and he'll fall to his death.

如果亨利继续玩跳伞，他很快会死亡。如果有一天他的降落伞没有打开，然后他就跳下去死了。

Teacher Josh If someone is pushing up daisies, it means they have died. Daises are a type of flower that sometimes grow in cemeteries. This is an informal expression to refer to anyone who is no longer alive or will soon not be alive. Similar euphemisms are "expired" and "kicked the bucket."

Daises 是雏菊，雏菊可以在墓地生长，pushing up daises 字面意思是堆放雏菊，实际意思很简单，就是死亡。这是非常委婉的表达死亡或即将死亡的短语。表示死亡的其他委婉语还有"expired"和"kick the bucket"。

Find (Get) one's sea legs
适应新环境

扫码看视频
Scan for video

It took me a while to get comfortable, to find my sea legs, but now I feel confident at our weekly meetings.

适应新的环境需要花费一段时间，现在我在周会上感觉自信了。

Teacher Josh

If you find or get your sea legs, you have the ability to walk steadily aboard a ship or boat. Figuratively, it means to successfully adjust to a new environment. In the above example, presenting at the weekly meetings initially made the speaker feel nervous, but he gained confidence over time and now feels comfortable.

Find one's sea legs，可不是找到你的海洋腿。Sea legs是航海用语，指的是在颠簸的船上能平稳行走而不晕船的能力，后来比喻"适应新环境"。例句中发言人起初参加周会感觉紧张，但是过了一段时间，她参会变得自信，适应了新环境。

Put a sock in it

别说了，闭嘴

扫码看视频
Scan for video

She would not stop talking nonsense, so I told her to put a sock in it.

她不停地胡说八道，所以我告诉她闭嘴，别说了。

Teacher Josh This expression is used to tell someone to stop talking. It implies that if one does not stop speaking, someone is going to stuff a sock in one's mouth. This originated in the early twentieth century, and although it does not sound very nice, it is often used humorously.

Put a sock in it 直译是"把袜子放进去"，实际意思是"闭嘴"。如果你不停止讲话，我就把袜子塞到你嘴里让你闭嘴。这不是一个礼貌的表达，但是很常用，这个习语在20世纪初期变得流行起来。

Catfishing

欺骗

She had a blind date with a guy who said he was 30, but when she showed up at the restaurant, he looked to be about 60. The old guy catfished her!

她和一位自称30岁的男士初次见面，但是当她出现在餐厅，他看上去60岁多。这个老男人欺骗了她。

扫码看视频
Scan for video

Teacher Josh This term is used to refer to someone presenting an identity online that is very different from who they really are so as to attract, and often cheat, another person.

Catfish是鲶鱼，一位渔民要去捕捞鲶鱼，我们叫做 catfishing。但是这里指的是另外一个意思，在社交媒体或网络上，假装自己是另外一个人，这个人比较帅，比较漂亮，比较有吸引力，通过欺骗的方式勾引另外一个人。这个习语在过去的十年或二十年变得流行起来。

Thick as thieves
非常亲密

扫码看视频
Scan for video

The three kids spent every moment they could together. They were as thick as thieves.

这三个小孩每天从早玩到晚在一起。他们非常亲密。

Teacher Josh This describes close friends. Here, "thick" means intimate or close. When two people are as thick as thieves, they spend a lot of time together and trust each other with secrets. This closeness is likened to the relationship of thieves who work together closely and in secret.

Thick 意思是"厚"，是thin的反义词。习语中的thick指的是亲密的，亲近的。当两个人thick as thieves，他们是非常亲密的，分享秘密，让其他人以为他们正在隐藏或者计划某事。直译是"像盗贼一样亲密"，实际意思形容非常亲密的朋友，共同分享秘密。

Ghost of a chance
机会渺茫

扫码看视频
Scan for video

The odds of Jim winning the lottery are a million to one. He doesn't have a ghost of a chance.

吉姆赢彩票的机会是百万分之一。他机会渺茫。

Teacher Josh This idiom, used to indicate a remote possibility, has appeared in print as early as 1857, in Thomas Hughes's *Tom Brown's School Days*. It is usually used in a negative sense to mean there is no chance whatsoever.

这个习语可以追溯到19世纪，在Thomas Hughes 写作的《Tom Brown's School Days》一书中出现。A ghost of a chance指的是机会很小，如果一个人说"have not a ghost of a chance"，意思是无论怎样都没有任何机会。

So far so good

到目前为止还不错

扫码看视频
Scan for video

I've covered 15 miles of the 26-mile marathon, and things are going well. So far, so good.

26英里的马拉松，我已经跑了15英里，一切进行的很顺利。到目前为止还不错。

Teacher Josh

This phrase indicates that the development of something is quite good or acceptable up to this time. It also implies that one hopes the situation continues smoothly, though one cannot be sure it will. This first appeared in James Kelly's *Scottish Proverbs* in 1721.

这个习语最早出现于1721年詹姆斯·凯利 (James Kelly)所著的《苏格兰谚语》 (Scottish Proverbs) 一书中，意思是当下这段时间内是满意的。暗指事情到目前为止进展的很顺利，但是接下来不一定会进展很顺利。

Out of the blue

突然；出乎意料地

扫码看视频
Scan for video

She was surprised to find her boyfriend unexpectedly back in town; he appeared at her door out of the blue.

当她听说她男朋友意外地返回小镇，突然出现，她惊呆了。

Teacher Josh This means unexpectedly. "Out of the clear blue sky" is a similar expression. It compares the suddenness of an event to lightning that unexpectedly flashes across the blue sky, strikes a tree and causes it to topple.

Blue指天空，Out of the blue意思是"像从天上掉下来一样"，翻译为"突然地，出乎意料地"。想象你正在享受着晴朗的天气，天空湛蓝而清澈，突然地，不知道从哪里来了一道闪电击中了一棵树，真是突如其来，晴天霹雳。这就是这个习语的来源。

Wipe the floor with someone
把某人打得一败涂地

The jockey on the #1 horse wiped the floor with the other jockeys by finishing way ahead of them in the race.

在 #1 的赛马骑师把其他的骑师们打败了，在比赛中提前到达终点。

扫码看视频
Scan for video

Teacher Josh This means to defeat an opponent comfortably and without much difficulty. According to *A Dictionary of Slang, Jargon and Cant* (1897), this comes from the idea that a loser has been knocked to the floor, and the winner can simply pick him up like a fallen broom or mop for cleaning the floor.

根据 Barrère and Leland 编写的俚语字典解释，意思是一个人把另一个人完全打倒在地，把一个人比喻成一个扫帚或抹布，把另一个人扫出去或擦掉。所以我们将 "To wipe the floor with someone" 翻译为打败一位对手。

Come rain or shine
风雨无阻

扫码看视频
Scan for video

We're having the party come rain or shine, whether Grandpa is able attend it or otherwise.

我们会风雨无阻地举行聚会，无论祖父是否来参加。

Teacher Josh This idiom means something will happen regardless of any changes to a situation. It is used figuratively to mean no matter what circumstances arise. For example, a woman who says to her husband, "I will always love you, come rain or shine," means she will love him no matter what.

这个习语的意思是无论下雨与否，一些活动都会举行。比喻无论发生什么事情，都无法阻止某事发生。举个例子，妻子对她的丈夫会说，"I will always love you, come rain or shine，"意思是无论发生什么，她都会永远爱他。

Desperate times call for drastic measures

危急时刻需要采取非常措施

扫码看视频
Scan for video

The general called for air support to save the lives of his troops. Desperate times call for drastic measures.

将军请求空军支援来拯救他的部队成员。危机时刻需要采取非常措施。

Teacher Josh This saying is derived from Greek physician Hippocrates, who described how taking unusually bold actions in the face of extremely difficult conditions is necessary. For example, during the COVID-19 outbreak, governments around the world took extreme measures to control the spread of the virus.

这个习语来自于古希腊名医——希波克拉底 (Hippocrates)，在他的格言中提及到。Desperate times call for drastic measures意思是在危难时刻，有必要采取严厉的，极端的措施。比如，在传染病面前，政府采取严厉的措施控制疾病的扩散。危急时刻需要采取非常措施。

Crack a book

打开书阅读

扫码看视频
Scan for video

He passed the exam without even studying — he didn't even crack a book.

他没有学习就通过了考试，他还没有打开书阅读。

Teacher Josh To crack a book means to open one and read or study it. This idiom, which gained popularity in the eighteenth century, is often used negatively to describe someone who has not opened a book to study.

To crack a book 在18世纪变得流行起来，简单来说就是打开一本书，然后阅读，通常用在消极的情况下。比如说，你不想看书，但是由于准备考试不得不读书，这种情况下就可以使用该习语。

No picnic
并非易事

扫码看视频
Scan for video

They had a tough flight with their new infant; it's no picnic trying to take care of a crying baby on a plane.

他们与他们刚出生的婴儿经历了一次艰难的旅行；在飞机上照顾一个哭闹的宝贝并非易事。

Teacher Josh If something is no picnic, it is a difficult or unpleasant experience. A broken leg, for example, is no picnic. This expression was first recorded in 1888.

这个习语最早记录是在1888年，在晴朗的天气户外野餐（picnic）很美好。那么 no picnic 和野餐关系不大，指的是一次经历或一次活动不愉快，很艰难。比方说，折断腿就是 no picnic。

Throw someone under the bus
故意害人

扫码看视频
Scan for video

I saw Jane write a curse word on the blackboard, so I threw her under the bus by reporting it to our teacher.

我看见简在黑板上写了一个诅咒的单词，然后我告诉我们老师，我故意害简。

Teacher Josh If you throw someone under a bus, it means you do something harmful to someone to gain advantage for yourself. For example: "He wants the job so much that he'll throw anyone under the bus to get it."

To throw someone under the bus 字面意思看是把某人推到公交车下面，实际上这是一个比喻。这个习语的意思是为了达到自己的目的或者获利，做一些对别人伤害的事情，故意害人。比如，一个人很想得到一份工作，为了得到这份工作，他会故意伤害别人，甚至背叛或出卖。这个习语自2004年以来被运动新闻记者较多使用。

You can't judge a book by its cover
不要以貌取人

扫码看视频
Scan for video

I was surprised to learn that the gruff-looking man was very friendly. This just proves that you can't judge a book by its cover.

我很惊奇的发现这位长得粗鲁的男士很友好。恰好验证了不要以貌取人。

Teacher Josh

This has been a common saying since the mid-1800s. It is often used to describe how you are unable to know someone's character based on their appearance. Sometimes, however, it's used to describe things other than people. For example: "That dingy-looking restaurant serves the best food I've ever eaten. You can't judge a book by its cover!"

You can't judge a book by its cover意思是不可以仅凭一个人外貌去判断一个人。有时候这个习语也用来描写某件物品。比如你到访一间很小很脏的餐厅，但是发现食物是你吃过最好吃的，这么小的低级餐馆竟然可以提供这么美味食物，这时你可以使用这个习语去表达。这个表达白19世纪中期便开始使用了。

Leave no stone unturned
千方百计；用尽一切手段

The police examined the photographs of all the suspects over and over again. They left no stone unturned.

警察一遍又一遍的检查了每一位嫌疑犯的照片。他们用尽一切手段。

扫码看视频
Scan for video

Teacher Josh

This means to do everything possible, especially when looking for something, to achieve a good result. The idiom comes from the legend of a Greek general who had buried some treasure before he died in battle. Those searching for it were advised by the Oracle of Delphi to look under every stone.

这个习语来源于古希腊神话。相传，有一位将军战败后潜逃，在军队驻地埋了宝藏，寻宝藏的人找不到便向特尔斐神 (Oracle of Delphi) 询问，神谕提示他们要 "leave no stone unturned"，即 "一块石头也不留地翻过来。" 现引申为千方百计，一个人为了完成目标，用尽一切方法，特别指寻找某些东西。

Head over heels
对某人神魄颠倒

扫码看视频
Scan for video

He fell madly in love with his girlfriend on the day he met her; he was head over heels in love.

他从遇到她的那天就疯狂的爱上了她女朋友；他对她神魂颠倒。

Teacher Josh This idiom describes being completely in love with someone or something. The original expression was "heels over head," referring to someone who had taken a serious fall, causing him to end up with his heels above his head. The order of "heels" and "head" was flipped in the eighteenth century.

Head over heels 字面意思是头在高跟鞋上面，显然这没有什么异议。然而，几百年前这个习语是 "heels over head"，鞋子在头上面，意思是一个人摔倒了，头朝下，鞋朝上。到18世纪末期，习语又反过来了，变成了"head over heels"，原因可能是作者弄错了。该习语现在多指深深的爱上了一个人，坠入情网，神魂颠倒。

Hit the road
出发

I have to leave to catch the bus, I'm ready to hit the road.

我必须离开去乘坐公共汽车，我准备好出发了。

扫码看视频
Scan for video

Teacher Josh To hit the road means to be on one's way, to leave a place or set out on a journey. Originally this common expression referred to horses hitting the road with their hooves. Presently, it alludes to a person's foot or the tires of a vehicle coming into contact with the road.

Hit the road 可不是敲打路，也不是修路的意思，而是准备好上路了，离开一个地方，开始一段旅程。是谁hit the road呢？这里指某人的双脚或者是汽车轮胎 hit the road。这个习语的起源与马有关，马用蹄子踏路出行。这是一个非常常用的习语，和"time to get going"同义。

On cloud nine

极其快乐

扫码看视频
Scan for video

I was so happy on my wedding day, I felt like I was on cloud nine.

婚礼那天我感觉很幸福，极其快乐。

Teacher Josh To be on cloud nine means to be extremely happy. Its origins are uncertain, but it is possibly based on information in the *International Cloud Atlas*, published in 1896. The atlas references ten cloud types, with cumulonimbus, the biggest and puffiest, labelled as No. 9.

On cloud nine 从字面看是"在九重云霄上"，这个习语的起源不是很确定，但有一种说法和云层有关系。在1896年国际云图集中讲到有十种类型云，其中第九层是最大的，最松软的，最舒适的。所以现在用来形容非常开心，极其快乐，放佛置身九霄云外。

Grease monkey
汽车检修工

扫码看视频
Scan for video

I work on cars day and night. I'm a grease monkey.

我每天从早到晚修理汽车。我是一名汽车检修工。

Teacher Josh

A grease monkey is a mechanic, someone who maintains and repairs machinery, usually motor vehicles. This expression may have come from the Industrial Revolution in Great Britain, when children were hired to grease the large rotating axles used to transfer power from steam engines to factory machines.

A grease monkey，也叫机修工（mechanic）。这个习语可以追溯到1928年，和英国的工业革命有关，那时小伙们习惯了往旋转轴上面涂油脂（grease），这个旋转轴可以将蒸汽发动机的动力传送到工厂地面上的 所有机器。现在 grease monkey 指机修工，尤其指检修汽车工人。

Time is money

一寸光阴一寸金

扫码看视频
Scan for video

Jim is wasting his time watching TV all day instead of looking for a job. He doesn't understand that time is money.

吉姆全天浪费时间看电视，而不是去找工作。他不懂得一寸光阴一寸金。

Teacher Josh This expression was coined by Benjamin Franklin, one of the Founding Fathers of the USA, in 1748. "Remember that time is money," he wrote, implying that to earn money, one must act and therefore use one's time efficiently and productively.

这个习语来自本杰明·富兰克林，美国建国领袖之一。他于1748年在一本书中写道"Remember that time is money"，意思是为了赚钱，一个人必须行动起来，充分利用有限的时间。如果高效的利用时间，你会很快赚到钱；如果你虚度光阴，你就徒劳无功。

A bird in the hand is worth two in the bush

一鸟在手，胜过两鸟在林

He left the poker table with his winnings instead of risking it to win more because a bird in the hand is worth two in the bush.

他带着赢的的钱离开扑克桌，而不是拿这些钱冒险去赢更多，因为一鸟在手，胜过两鸟在林。

扫码看视频
Scan for video

Teacher Josh This saying first appeared in English in 1530. It means it is better to be satisfied with the certainty of having something of less value than to pursue the possibility of a something more valuable that may come to nothing. It dates to medieval falconry, in which a bird in the hand (the falcon) was more valuable than two in the bush (the prey).

这个习语，最早于1530年在英语中出现，字面意思是"比起丛林中的两只鸟，手中的一只鸟更有价值。"这个习语来源于中世纪放鹰捕猎，比起丛林中的两只猎物，手中的一只鹰就是有价值的财产。喻指要珍惜现在拥有的一切，抓住现在，而不是去赌未来，未来可能一无所获。

No dice
没门儿；不行

Bob asked to join the team, but I said no dice because he was too young.

鲍勃请求加入团队，但是我说不行，因为他太年轻了。

扫码看视频
Scan for video

Teacher Josh If someone declares "no dice," they mean that there is no chance for something. It can be used to express rejection or to show failure in an attempt. For example: "We tried to find a room at the hotel, but no dice; it was fully booked at this time of year." The phrase originated in the USA in the early twentieth century.

Dice 是骰子，No dice 就是不用掷骰子，不赞同，没门儿，不可能。比如你要去某地度假，可以这么说"We tried to find a room at the hotel, but no dice, it was fully booked at this time of the year."意思是不可能找到空房间了，今年这个时节全订满了。这个习语起源于20世纪早期的美国。

Easy does it (Take it easy)
别着急；小心行事

You just broke your foot, you shouldn't be running around. Take it slowly. Easy does it.

你脚刚刚骨折了，你不应该到处跑。慢慢来。别着急。

扫码看视频
Scan for video

Teacher Josh This expression was used to urge people not to worry about the next day because any problem or task will present itself when the day arrives. When someone says, "easy does it," they are asking the listener to do something slowly and carefully.

"Easy does it"可不是说"容易做"，而是说慢慢做，别着急；仔细认真做，小心行事。这个习语首次使用是在《圣经》新的圣约，告诉人们不用杞人忧天，比如有人要搬放瓷器古董，你可以对他说"It's fragile. Easy does it."意思是"这个易碎，要小心，别着急。"

Your guess is as good as mine

我也不知道

扫码看视频
Scan for video

We're both unclear about the situation, so your guess
is as good as mine.

我们都不清楚情况，所以我也不知道。

Teacher Josh This phrase means that you are not sure of the answer to a question. You can take a guess, but you are really unsure. This expression is used in everyday conversation. Its origins are unclear.

这个习语直译是"你的猜想和我一样"，实际意思是"我也不知道"。你对某事不确定，所以可以猜一猜（guess）。"Your guess is as good as mine"非常常用，但是它的起源不详。

Go on a wild goose chase
白费力气

扫码看视频
Scan for video

The search is pointless — they will never find anything. It's a wild goose chase.

这项探究是没有意义的，他们永远不会发现任何情况。
真是白费力气。

Teacher Josh If you go on a wild goose chase, you are going on a search or attempting to do something that is likely to end in disappointment. This idiom dates to the sixteenth century and was used to describe a horse race in which one rider in front would be chased by others. This resembled how geese fly in formation by following a lead.

"Go on a wild goose chase"字面意思理解是"追上一群野雁"，表示"白费力气"，相当于谚语"竹篮打水一场空"。这个习语起源于16世纪的骑马比赛，骑马比赛的第一名被其他骑师追随，就像编队飞行的大雁首领一样，所以说goose chase（追雁）。

Method to my madness
看似疯狂的举动其实是有目的的

You may think I'm disorganized, but as crazy as it looks, I know what I'm doing; there is a method to my madness.

你可能认为我不按常理出牌，虽然看似疯狂，但是我知道我在做什么。看似疯狂的举动其实是有目的的。

扫码看视频
Scan for video

Teacher Josh: This is one of the many memorable expressions coined by Shakespeare that has become commonplace. Taken from *Hamlet* (c.1602), it means there is a plan behind what someone is doing, even if it is not immediately apparent.

这个习语出自1602年莎士比亚创作的的《哈姆雷特》，意思是一个人做事情的背后有一个计划，尽管这个计划可能不明显。有些行为看上去难以理喻，但是这样做是有原因的。看下面这个例子："At the start of his presentation, it seemed that he was out of his mind, but when he finished, we saw that there's method to his madness。"在他演讲之初有些疯狂，但是当结束的时候，我们发现看似疯狂的行动其实是有目的的。

A penny saved is a penny earned
省钱就是赚钱

Please put this money in the bank and then you'll have even more when you need it. A penny saved is a penny earned.

请把钱存入银行，如果当你需要的时候你会有更多钱。省钱就是赚钱。

扫码看视频
Scan for video

Teacher Josh: The phrase means it is just as useful to save the money that you already have as it is to earn more, so don't waste your earnings. It is based on a similar expression found in Benjamin Franklin's *Poor Richard's Almanack*.

这个习语来源于本杰明·富兰克林写的一本书《Poor Richard's Almanack》。A penny 指的是一便士，一分钱。不要小看这个一分钱，A penny saved is a penny earned，说的是省下一分钱，相当于多赚一分钱。简言之就是不要浪费钱，而是要存钱。

Granddaddy of them all
史上之最

I've seen a lot of crazy glasses, but Larry's are the granddaddy of them all.

我看到过很多疯狂的眼镜，但是拉里的眼镜是史上最疯狂的。

扫码看视频
Scan for video

Teacher Josh This describes something as the first, oldest or most extreme of its kind. For example: "That was the granddaddy of all hurricanes," the weatherman said. This means that the hurricane referred to was the biggest and fiercest ever recorded.

Granddad，相当于grandpa，是爷爷的意思。Granddaddy可翻译为祖师爷。如果我们说某事物"granddaddy of them all"，意思指的是某人或某事在一个领域或区域内是最早的，最大的，最有影响力的。举例"That was the granddaddy of all hurricanes, according to the weather forecaster。"意思是这次飓风是历史上最大最强劲的一次。

For a song
非常便宜地

扫码看视频
Scan for video

She bought that antique chest for a song. It was definitely worth more than $200.

她非常便宜地买了古董。这个价值可不止200美金。

Teacher Josh If you buy something for a song, you have purchased it very cheaply. This phrase gained popularity in the seventeenth century, and likely comes from the practice of selling written song sheets for very low prices at fairs at that time.

For a song 字面意思是"为了一首歌"，实则不然。以前，在集市上售卖写的民歌剧本是很便宜的，所以for a song用来指非常便宜地，相当廉价地。这个表达在17世纪中期流行起来。

Get (start) off on the wrong foot
一开始就不顺利

扫码看视频
Scan for video

Peggy got off on the wrong foot with her new teacher on the first day of class by chewing gum.

佩吉给她的新老师留下了不好的印象，因为她在第一节课上嚼口香糖，尽管不被允许。

Teacher Josh
To get off on the wrong foot means to start something badly. It is usually used to describe a relationship or project. This expression may come from an old superstition that the left side of the body is linked to bad luck, so the "wrong foot" is the left foot.

To get off on the wrong foot 直译是"开始迈错脚"。这里的wrong foot指的是左脚，古代有种迷信说人身体的左侧和不好的运气挂钩，罗马人有时会在公共建筑物的门口安排保安，以确保进入的人先迈右脚，而不是左脚。延伸的意思就是"一开始就不顺利"。多指某人一开始就没给人一个好印象，相处关系不好；或一开始由于某种行为而把事情弄糟了，出师不利。

Have a bite
吃点东西

扫码看视频
Scan for video

They did not want to ruin their appetite for dinner, so they had just a bite for lunch.

他们不想破坏晚餐进食，所以午餐他们仅吃了一点东西。

Teacher Josh To have a bite is to eat a small portion of food, like a snack or a small meal, and usually in a quick fashion. For example: "Let's have a bite before we hit the road." This means let's have a snack before starting our journey.

Bite是"咬"的意思，Have a bite可不是咬一口，而是"吃点东西，吃点小吃，很快地吃完"。举例，"Let's get a bite before we hit the road。"意思是在出发之前简单吃一点。Hit the road指的是出发，在本书前面提到过。

Extra pair of hands

额外的帮手

It's really helpful to have an extra pair of hands, to have everyone pitch in, when you're painting your house.

当你粉刷房子的时候，让所有人出力，有额外的帮手帮忙是真的有帮助的。

扫码看视频
Scan for video

Teacher Josh An extra pair of hands means someone who can provide additional assistance. When one offers help to another person, one often uses their hands in the process.

An extra pair of hands 简单来说就是某人可以提供帮助。当一个人提供帮助通常会使用他的手，比如说粉刷房子或者搬重的物品或做任何其他人工工作。

Speak of the devil

说曹操，曹操到

Speak of the devil! I was just talking about you.

说曹操，曹操到！我刚刚谈及到你。

扫码看视频
Scan for video

Teacher Josh This phrase is used to express surprise when someone you're talking about shows up unexpectedly. The phrase comes from medieval England, where people were superstitious and almost never spoke directly of the Devil for fear that it would incite him to appear.

这个习语起源于英国中世纪，那时人们迷信，几乎从不和魔鬼对话，害怕这样做会鼓动魔鬼出现，造成不幸的后果。"Speak of the devil" 现在指谈话中谈到某人，结果这个人突然出现了。

In the heat of the moment
一时激动

I was so anxious to get home that in the heat of the moment I did not see the traffic sign warning of a sharp curve ahead.

我特别急切的想回家，一时激动，我没有看到急转弯的标志。

扫码看视频
Scan for video

Teacher Josh This expression means to act out suddenly with passion, often in anger. Such moments are often regretted later. For example, an employee might yell at her boss in the heat of the moment and later regret it.

如果说某人做某事"in the heat of the moment"，指这个人是在生气或激动的情况下，没有考虑后果地做了某事，之后却后悔这么做。比如一位员工可能会对他的老板喊叫，之后就会后悔。这个习语自20世纪后半叶便开始使用了。

Hear on the grapevine
道听途说

扫码看视频
Scan for video

She asked if I was certain our neighbors were getting a divorce. I said I had heard it on the grapevine and couldn't be sure.

她问我是否确定我们邻居已经离婚了，我说我只是道听途说，但是不确定。

Teacher Josh To hear something on the grapevine is to be told unverified news informally – a rumor. This saying comes from the American Civil War period when telegraph wires looked like vines, as they were hung and connected from tree to tree.

Grapevine指葡萄树，"hear it on the grapevine"直译"在葡萄树上听到"，在葡萄树上或通过葡萄藤听到的消息不能确定准确，一般指谣言或小道消息，非正式信息，通常是口头的消息。这个习语起源于美国内战时期由于技术不发达，那时电报机电线挂在树上，密密麻麻，像极了葡萄藤，所以习语才说 hear it on the grapevine。

Give someone the benefit of the doubt
对某人有怀疑，宁可暂时相信

扫码看视频
Scan for video

Even though she has lied in the past, I'm giving her the benefit of the doubt. I'm assuming that she is telling the truth.

我想相信她，尽管她过去撒过谎，所以我宁可暂时相信她。我假定她讲的是真话。

Teacher Josh This means to believe someone for the time being — usually about their claims of being innocent — even though you cannot be certain what the person is saying is true. For example: "I am not sure if he stole money, but I'm giving him the benefit of the doubt." This means that for now, without evidence proving guilt, you will accept that he is innocent.

这个习语指：尽管你不确定某人说的话是否正确，暂时相信他的话。举例，"I am not sure if he stole the money, but I'm giving him the benefit of the doubt."（我不确定他是否偷了钱，但是我宁可暂时相信他。）意思是你没有证据证明他偷了钱，所以你假定他没有偷。

Tie one on
宿醉后继续喝

He was so drunk last night that he was falling all over the place. He really tied one on.

他昨晚喝醉了，结果醉的一塌糊涂。他真的喝醉的。

Teacher Josh
This means to get drunk. The phrase is thought to date back to the the 1800s in the American Wild West, where a person would tie his horse to a hitching post, so that he could have drinks in a saloon.

Tie one on据说来源和19世纪西部地区的牛仔男孩有关，他在进入酒吧喝酒喝醉之前，会把他的马系在马桩上。所以用tie one on来形容喝醉酒，尤指第一天喝醉了，第二天宿醉（hangover），尽管醒来很难受，还继续喝酒，喝的一塌糊涂。

Get the hang of it
掌握窍门

It was tough learning how to play golf at first, but now I am getting the hang of it!

刚开始学习很困难，但是现在我逐步学会打高尔夫了，我正在掌握窍门。

扫码看视频
Scan for video

Teacher Josh

To get the hang of is to acquire a sense of how to do something properly, which means one will likely improve. In the mid-1800s attaching a handle to an axe was called "hanging." After practicing several times, a person will know how to position the handle perfectly on the axe head – doing so would be to "get the hang of it."

这个习语和19世纪中期制作一把斧头有关系，把斧头的手柄安装到斧头上的过程称为 "hanging"，安装几次之后，你开始发现怎么才能正好把手柄安装到斧头的头部，最终掌握窍门后，你可以说 "get the hang of [how to do] it"，这就是习语的来源。To get the hang of something 指的是获得或掌握做某事的窍门。

Catch some rays
晒太阳

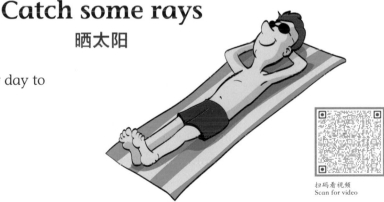

Billy goes to the beach every day to catch some rays.

比利每天去沙滩晒太阳。

扫码看视频
Scan for video

Teacher Josh

This means spend some leisure time in sunlight, usually to get a suntan. The rays refers to the rays of the sun. "Get some rays" also has the same meaning.

Catch some rays 意思是坐在太阳下，通常指享受日光浴的放松。Ray 指的是太阳光线，指阳光。"Get some rays"和"Catch some rays"是同一个意思。

All over the map
漫无目的，混乱无序

扫码看视频
Scan for video

The meeting today was all over the map; we did not stick to the main topic.

今天的会议混乱无序；我们没有坚持住主要的话题。

Teacher Josh This describes someone whose thinking is disorganized or incoherent. For example: "He couldn't understand her business proposal. It didn't make sense. She kept talking about different topics; she was all over the map."

All over the map 指的是一种毫无秩序或混乱的状态。如果说一次讨论all over the map，那就是脱离主题。如果说一个人针对某一个问题没有讲清楚也可以用all over the map，这个人思路不清晰，没有能力讲清楚。举例，"He couldn't understand her business proposal. It didn't make sense. She kept talking about all different topics; she was all over the map。"意思是她没有清晰的观点，没有表达清楚，反而让人迷惑。

Under one's thumb
受某人支配

扫码看视频
Scan for video

Billy is under his wife's thumb. She completely controls him.

比利受他的妻子支配。她完全地控制他。

Teacher Josh To be under one's thumb is to be constantly controlled or managed by someone else. It is unclear why the thumb was singled out as a symbol of control or power, but it has been so since the mid-1700s.

Thumb是大拇指的意思，猜测大拇指被认为是权利和控制的象征，所以"to be under one's thumb"引申意思是"完全地受某人控制，听命于他人"。这个习语自18世纪中期便出现。

Pull the plug

停止；终止

扫码看视频
Scan for video

Jimmy pulled the plug on the basketball game. In the middle of the game, he stopped abruptly and left.

吉米终止了正在进行的篮球比赛，他在比赛进行中放弃，然后突然回家。

Teacher Josh This means to stop something from continuing, usually abruptly. Think of what happens when you pull out a lamp plug from a socket; the power supply gets cut off and the lights go out. This expression became popular in the 1920s.

Pull the plug 字面意思是"拔出插头"，想一下如果你把一个灯的插销拔下来，灯不通电肯定没有灯光，光消失了，停止了。现在 pull the plug 意思是停止，多指终止一项活动或项目，比如一个商业项目或一个节目的录制。这个表达在20世纪20年代流行起来，但是起源不详。

A blessing in disguise
塞翁失马，焉知非福

扫码看视频
Scan for video

Missing the train for work was a blessing in disguise because with the extra time he was able to attend his son's baseball game.

错过了去工作的火车原来是塞翁失马，焉知非福。因为他可以空出时间去参加他儿子的棒球比赛。

Teacher Josh This phrase, which originated in the eighteenth century, describes a misfortune that eventually results in something useful or beneficial. In other words, something that seems bad at first but turns out to be good.

Blessing是好事的意思，disguise是伪装、掩饰。A blessing in disguise意思是原以为是倒霉的事，可结果证明反倒是件好事。这个表达起源于18世纪，并且在现代口语中经常使用。

Jump ship
离职

Harry unexpectedly quit the band. He jumped ship with no notice.

哈利竟然离开乐队了。他没通知就离职了。

扫码看视频
Scan for video

Teacher Josh: This saying means to leave an organization or group, or to distance oneself from a movement, usually in an abrupt manner. It is derived from a sailor wanting to leave his ship without permission. He would jump overboard near land and swim to shore, abandoning his post and the ship.

Jump ship 字面意思是"跳船"，在古代，水手未经授权想要离开，他们会在船快靠岸的时候，跳下船游到岸边，所以jump ship就是离开岗位，抛弃那艘船。我们习惯说一个团队的人，叫做同一条船上的人，如果说跳船，就是指离开一个组织或团体，跳槽的意思。

Drive (someone) up the wall
使发疯；使烦恼

Jane drove Sally up the wall by constantly requesting to borrow her car.

简不断的请求借萨莉的车，快把萨莉逼疯了。

扫码看视频
Scan for video

Teacher Josh: This means to make someone irritated or angry. The saying evokes the image of someone trying desperately to get away from someone or something by climbing over a wall. It is not clear when this idiom came to use.

"Drive someone up the wall"字面意思是促使某人往墙上爬，实际意思相当于汉语中的"把某人逼上梁山"，某事或某人让人烦恼生气，让人发疯。这个习语何时最早使用没有明确记载。

Smell a rat
怀疑有问题

I could see from the way Henry was shuffling the cards that he was cheating. I smelled a rat.

我看到亨利在洗牌时作弊。
我怀疑有问题。

扫码看视频
Scan for video

Teacher Josh This describes recognizing that something dishonest is happening. The expression comes from the days when rats were common pests and a dog was prized for its ability to sniff out and destroy them. It later came to mean to be suspicious of something.

Smell a rat，字面意思是"闻到一只老鼠"，而真正意思是"怀疑某事不像看上去的那样，感觉事情不妙"。这个习语的来源和老鼠（rat）有关，老鼠被普遍认为是害虫，狗擅长用鼻子闻到老鼠的踪迹，捉住老鼠。同理，"smell a rat"指人感到事情不对劲，怀疑某事有问题。

Give props to
向某人表示感谢

We would like to thank and give props to those who have helped us tonight.

我们要向今晚帮助我们的那些人表示感谢。

扫码看视频
Scan for video

Teacher Josh This American expression originated in the 1980s and means to give proper recognition to someone or proclaim respect for them. It is often implied that the acknowledgement and praise is overdue. By example: "He gave props to his wife and children for their ongoing support."

这个习语起源于美国20世纪80年代。prop 是支持的意思，give props to指对某人表示支持，表示感谢，表示一直以来的尊重。举例，"He gave props to his wife and kids for their ongoing support."（他对他老婆和孩子一直以来的支持表示感谢。）

Night owl
夜猫子

扫码看视频
Scan for video

Billy enjoys evenings much more than daytime. He's a night owl.

比利喜欢晚上多于白天。他是一个夜猫子。

Teacher Josh

A night owl is a person who tends to stay up late at night or even into the early hours of the day. Many owls are known to be nocturnal, which means they are active during the night.

A night owl 意思是夜猫子，形容一个人倾向于熬夜到很晚，甚至熬夜到早上。这个习语来自于它的字面意思，owl 是猫头鹰，猫头鹰是夜间动物，晚上醒着，白天睡觉。

Devil's advocate
唱反调

扫码看视频
Scan for video

That teacher always presents a controversial opinion just to start a debate. He loves to play devil's advocate.

那位教师总是提出一个争议观点引发一次争论。他喜欢唱反调。

Teacher Josh

This describes someone who supports an opposing or unpopular cause for the sake of argument. The term comes from *advocatus diabolo*, Latin for "one who advocates the contrary side." In the past, as part of declaring a deceased person as a saint, the Catholic Church appointed a person known as a devil's advocate to argue against the proposed canonization.

A devil's advocate 形容一个人支持相反的或不受欢迎的观点导致争论风险。这个习语来源于拉丁语 "*advocatus diabolo*"，大意是支持相反观点的人。几百年前，a devil's advocate 是天主教堂的一个人，他的工作是劝大家反对一个圣徒成为圣者。

Worth one's salt
称职的；胜任的

The detective proved that she was worth her salt and deserving of her new raise by closing more cases than any other detective in the city.

这个警探证明她是称职的，加薪是值得的，因为与城市中其他的警探相比，她抓到了更多人。

扫码看视频
Scan for video

Teacher Josh This means to be good at one's job and deserving of one's pay or reward. In Roman times, salt was highly prized, so soldiers were given an allowance called a "salarium" to purchase salt. This gave rise to the modern word "salary."

在古罗马时期，盐是非常珍贵的。军人的工资的一部分就是盐，后来慢慢演变，发盐也变成了发购盐证券(salarium)。 这个词后来演变成了salary （工资）。英语中说 worth one's salt 指的是"某人很称职"。

A mile a minute
很快

扫码看视频
Scan for video

She was talking a mile a minute, so quickly that even her mom could not understand her.

她说得很快，特别快甚至她的妈妈不能理解她。

Teacher Josh This expression, which describes doing something very quickly, such as speaking rapidly, dates from the mid-1900s. It alludes to a car moving at the speed of 60 miles per hour — in the past this was considered a high speed.

Mile是英里，字面意思是"一分钟一英里"，这个表达追溯到20世纪中期，通常形容速度会用到"公里/时"，开车每小时六十英里，在当时这个速度是非常快的。所以如果说某人 talk a mile a minute，指说话很快。

Fish out of water
与周围的人或环境格格不入

Carl had never before visited a large city. He felt uncomfortable, and was like a fish out of water.

卡尔之前从来没有去过一个大城市。他感觉不舒服，与周围的人或环境格格不入。

扫码看视频
Scan for video

Teacher Josh A person who is a fish out of water is someone who feels uncomfortable because they are in a new situation or environment. When fish arc out of water, they are not in their usual environment and struggle to breathe. This expression was used by Geoffrey Chaucer to describe a character who is uncomfortable when riding a horse.

Fish out of water 字面意思是"离水之鱼"，鱼离开水不能呼吸，很快会窒息。现在多形容某人在不熟悉的环境下感觉不舒服。这个表达追溯到1483年，当时作家Geoffrey Chaucer使用这个习语形容骑马感觉不舒服的人。

Two peas in a pod
一模一样；形影不离

Tony and Angela are like two peas in a pod; they're always together.

托尼和安吉拉就像一个豆荚里的两颗豌豆；他们总是形影不离。

扫码看视频
Scan for video

Teacher Josh This expression is used to describe two people who are similar in appearance or behavior. Two peas inside of a pod look very alike, so it's difficult to tell one apart from the other.

Pea是豌豆，pod是豆荚，two peas in a pod字面意思是"一个豆荚里有两个豌豆"。这个短语非常形象，豆荚里的两颗豌豆几乎一样，你能区分出来吗？事实上很难，因为他们几乎一模一样。通常用来形容两个人长得像，或者性格、性情及兴趣相投，有很多相似点，亲密无间，形影不离。

Take the cake
无人能敌

扫码看视频
Scan for video

That is the most remarkable and foolish opinion Jake has ever uttered. It really takes the cake.

那是杰克发表的最为非凡的和愚蠢的的观点。真是无人能敌。

Teacher Josh This means to be above others in an extreme way. It can be used positively but is usually used to refer to a negative quality. By example: "His arrogance takes the cake," means that nobody can be more arrogant than this person. The ancient Greeks used the word "cake" to mean a symbolic prize.

Take the cake 一语双关。起初，小孩子玩游戏，胜利了得到饼干作为奖励，所以就用 take the cake 表示"得头奖，最出色的人或事"。后来，take the cake 演变为"超过某人"，尤指在不好的方面超过其他所有人。比如，如果你说"His arrogance takes the cake"，意思是没有人比他更自大了，他是最自大的，这是一种讽刺。现在多用来指：在不好的方面超过其他人，无人能敌，含有讽刺的意蕴。

175

Better late than never
迟做总比不做好

扫码看视频
Scan for video

Mom was late picking me up from school but I was glad to see her when she arrived. Better late than never.

妈妈去学校接我迟到了，但是当她来了我看到她时很开心。迟做总比不做好。

Teacher Josh Better late than never means finishing something later than planned is preferable to not finishing it at all. Its first known use is in "The Yeoman's Tale" from Geoffrey Chaucer's *The Canterbury Tales*, which dates back to the fourteenth century.

据记载，这个习语最早使用追溯到1386年，来自Chaucer's 《Canterbury Tales》的 "The Yeoman's Tale"。意思是比起计划的时间迟到做，总比不做好。

In the same boat
处境相同

We're all stuck in this elevator together. We're in the same boat!

我们现在都困在电梯上了。我们处境相同。

扫码看视频
Scan for video

Teacher Josh This describes a situation, usually negative, in which several people are trapped together. Taken from the ancient Greeks, this expression comes from how people sailing in the same boat share the same risk until they arrive at their destination. Over the years, the meaning has extended to mean all who face the same trouble.

In the same boat 并不是说真的在同一艘船上。这个习语源于古希腊，在同一艘船上的乘客在他们到达目的地之前，会分担相同的风险。后来逐渐的延伸为：处在相同困境中的人们，不管是在船上还是在大陆，与中文中的"在同一条绳子上的蚂蚱"类似。

Paint the town red
纵情狂欢

I told Sal to celebrate in a flamboyant way, to go out and paint the town red!

我告诉萨尔外出并以炫耀的方式庆祝，纵情狂欢。

扫码看视频
Scan for video

Teacher Josh This idiom describes a reckless spree. While its origins are disputed, some say that it dates to 1837, when the third Marquess of Waterford and a group of his friends covered a number of buildings with red paint in Melton Mowbray, a small English town.

Paint是涂画，town是小镇，有人将paint the town red 翻译为把小镇涂成红色，字面意思确实是这样的，但实际意思是花天酒地的玩乐，纵情狂欢。这个习语起源于1837年，在英国有一个叫 Melton Mowbray 的小镇，一个臭名昭著的人叫Marquess of Waterford，他和他的朋友们在镇上发动暴乱，把镇上的酒吧和建筑物粉刷成红色。

Time flies when you're having fun
开心的时候感觉时间过得很快

When I'm in my workshop, time seems to move unbelievably fast. It's true that time flies when you're having fun.

当我在工作室的时候，时间感觉过得不可思议的快。开心的时候感觉时间过得很快。

扫码看视频
Scan for video

Teacher Josh
This expression describes how time seems to pass quickly when you are engaged in something enjoyable. It was first recorded in 1800, though Shakespeare and Alexander Pope had used similar phrases earlier.

这个习语的意思是当你从事一项有趣的活动时，时间过得很快。这个习语最早记录约在1800年，莎士比亚用了一个相似的表达"the swiftest hours, as they flew"，亚历山大·蒲柏也用到"swift fly the years"表达。

Call it a day
收工；到此结束

扫码看视频
Scan for video

Okay, we have done as much as we can for now, so let's stop working and head home. Let's call it a day.

好吧，我们现在已经尽我们所能的做了很多，让我们停止工作回家吧。今天到此结束了。

Teacher Josh
This phrase means to stop doing something. It is used when people have been working a long time and are either too tired, hungry, or it's too late to make any progress on the task at hand.

这个习惯用语源于1838年，最早用的是"call it half a day"，那时工人们暂时完成工作，回家吃午餐，然后再返回完成他们的任务。到了1919年，出现了"call it a day"的说法，现在人们普遍指停止做某事，尤其指工作。通常人们工作了一整天，又累又饿，再工作也很难进步了，所以就下班，停止工作。

Wouldn't be caught dead
无论如何都不

扫码看视频
Scan for video

I wouldn't be caught dead wearing that shirt. I would never wear it.

我无论如何都不穿那个衬衫。我永远不会穿它。

Teacher Josh If you "wouldn't be caught dead" in something, or with someone, or somewhere, this means you really don't like the item, the person or the place. The above example shows how terrible the shirt seems to the person, and she is using this expression of extreme exaggeration to reject the shirt.

Wouldn't be caught dead 意思是你不喜欢某物，宁可死也不想做某事。例句中的意思就是说，"即使死了也不想让任何人看到我穿那件难看的衬衫"，一种夸张的方式形容衬衫非常难看。

Go down in flames
一败涂地

扫码看视频
Scan for video

Bill's grandfather was suddenly and completely ruined when the market crashed in 1929. He went down in flames.

1929年市场崩溃，比尔的祖父突然彻底地破产了。他一败涂地。

Teacher Josh You don't want to go down in flames as it indicates failing spectacularly. The phrase derived from World War II, when many combat planes that were shot and badly damaged would crash and burn. Today it can be used to describe a financial situation, a plan of action or project, or even negotiations.

这个习语作动词用，失败的很壮观，一败涂地，可以用来描述经济状况，一个计划或项目，甚至是谈判。比如，"The peace talks are sure to go down in flames"，指的就是和平谈判肯定会一败涂地。Go down in flames起源于1940年代，那时很多战斗飞机在二战中坠毁，飞机摧毁后会着火（go down in flames), 到地面燃烧起来。这就是该习语的起源。

Preaching to the choir
白费唇舌

扫码看视频
Scan for video

You're trying to make me agree that managing three kids is difficult, but I have three kids, so of course I agree! You're preaching to the choir.

你试着让我认可管理三个孩子很难，因为我有三个孩子我当然同意。你是白费唇舌。

Teacher Josh This saying, which became popular in the 1970s, means one is presenting an argument or opinion to others who already agree with it. Originally, it referred to the pointlessness of a preacher attempting to convert those who, by their presence in church, already believed in God.

如果说某人是 preaching to the choir，意思是他们正在陈述一个观点给一些人，而这些人实际上早就认可这个观点了，所以是白费唇舌。这个习语在20世纪70年代流行起来，有一位传教士向已经出现在教堂的人们传教，是毫无意义的，因为这些人已经认可信仰了。

Take with a grain of salt
怀疑某事，持保留态度

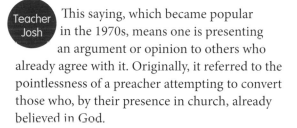
扫码看视频
Scan for video

I take what my co-worker Sam says with a grain of salt. I basically accept what he says, but I maintain a degree of skepticism.

我对我的合作伙伴山姆所说的持保留态度。我基本上同意他所说的，但是我保留一定程度怀疑。

Teacher Josh If you take what someone says with a grain of salt, you do not believe it is completely true. If you hear an unlikely story, it's like trying to eat bland food without spicing it up — add a little salt and it's easier to swallow.

"A grain of salt"，字面意思指一粒盐或一撮盐。Take something with a grain of salt 指的是对某事半信半疑，持保留态度。这个短语源于拉丁语 cum grano salis，与一个著名的古罗马传说有关。国王为了获得对毒物的免疫力，每天服用一个秘方，其中秘方里最后是一粒盐，因为盐可以帮助下咽。

Cry over spilt milk
覆水难收

Jan said she made a huge mistake not marrying Joe when she had the chance. I told to her to stop crying over spilt milk.

贾恩说她犯了一个巨大的错误，当机会来临时，她没有嫁给乔。我劝她别想了，覆水难收。

扫码看视频
Scan for video

Teacher Josh This means to regret or be upset about a mistake or problem that cannot be reversed or fixed. Welsh writer James Howell used the phrase "no weeping for shed milk" in his book *Paramoigraphy* (1659).

To cry over spilt milk 意思是：对于已经发生的不能改变的错误或问题，不要浪费时间悔恨莫及。有人说这习语第一次使用是在1888年出版的一本书中，故事讲述了一个人刚刚被抢劫了，尽管很窘迫，他回答说"It was no use, however, crying over spilt milk。"也有人说这个习语起源更早，是17世纪威尔士的作家James Howell在他的1659年箴言集（*Paramoigraphy*）中写到"no weeping for shed milk"。

Made of money
有钱

扫码看视频
Scan for video

I know you want the latest mobile phone but I'm not made of money — I can't afford it.

我知道你想要新的手机，但是我没有钱，我支付不起。

Teacher Josh If you describe someone as being made of money, it means that person is rich. This phrase, popular since the mid-1800s, is often used in the negative to deny a request for one to lend or spend money.

如果说某人 made of money，形容这个人很富。这个习语自19世纪开始流行，常用来拒绝别人，比如有人向你借钱，或者某人请你帮忙买某物，你可以说 I am not made of money，意思是我没有钱。

Zero to hero
从无到有

扫码看视频
Scan for video

Ken went from zero to hero when he won the lottery.

肯恩从无到有，在他中了彩票之后。

Teacher Josh This informal saying means to change one's situation significantly from negative to positive. It describes someone who, once unsuccessful, suddenly achieves success — or someone who, once unpopular, becomes popular.

From zero to hero 是一种非正式的表达，意思是一个人的处境改变了，从一无所有到成为英雄，从特别失败到特别成功。换句话说，一个人的运气显著的提升了，也指不流行变得流行起来。

At great length
详细而持久地

扫码看视频
Scan for video

The boring speaker rambled on at great length.
The lecture seemed like it would never end.

这位无聊的演说家详细而持久地讲着。看上去没有尽头。

Teacher Josh This means for a long duration and in great detail. By example: "The police interrogated the suspect at great length." This means the suspect was questioned for a long time. Do not confuse this with "go to great lengths," which means to make a major effort. "She went to great lengths to learn the truth."

At great length 是持久地、详细地意思。比如说，"The police interrogated the suspect at great length。"意思说警察盘问嫌疑犯很久，询问很多细节。注意不要与另一个习语混淆，"go to great lengths"是付出很多努力。比如，"She went to great lengths to learn the truth。"（她为了追寻真理做出了很多努力。）

Crocodile tears
假惺惺

She didn't really care that her teacher was ill, but she cried crocodile tears to make herself appear sensitive and kind.

她真的不在乎她老师病了，但是她假惺惺地哭了，使自己表面看上去善良。

扫码看视频
Scan for video

Teacher Josh This describes a display of sadness or regret that is not genuine. Crocodiles actually do shed tears when they're feeding, possibly because the tears clean their eyes. They may appear to be sad about killing their prey but the "crying" is no doubt insincere!

Crocodile tears 字面意思是"鳄鱼的眼泪"，凶猛的鳄鱼在惨忍地吞食弱小动物的时候会流眼泪，这并不是因为鳄鱼悔恨才流眼泪，而是一种自然的生理现象，目的在于排泄鳄鱼体内多余的盐分。所以产生了熟悉的"鳄鱼流眼泪"的说法，以此来比喻那些虚伪的坏人，假惺惺流眼泪。

Get wind of something
听到···的风声

扫码看视频
Scan for video

The police heard about a drug deal that was about to take place. They got wind of it from rumors on the street.

警察听说一次毒品交易将要发生。他们是从街上的谣言听到交易的风声。

Teacher Josh This phrase means to learn or hear about something that was not announced officially, usually because it was meant to be secret. It originated in the early 1800s and alludes to an animal becoming aware of others approaching due to their scent being carried over through the air.

Get wind of something 指听说某事，通常是通过传言或非正式的渠道。这个习语自19世纪上半叶开始使用，典故提及到一种动物可以从空气中感知一种气味，嗅到什么，现在指听到…风声，得到…秘密消息。

Out of the frying pan and into the fire
情况越来越糟

Children who run away from a troubled home usually find that they're out of the frying pan and into the fire once they're on their own.

孩子逃离了不安的家庭后，一旦他们依靠自己，会发现每况愈下。

扫码看视频
Scan for video

Teacher Josh This idiom means that in trying to escape from a bad or dangerous situation, one ends up in another situation that is worse than before. It is likely to have originated from a Greek saying about running from smoke into flames.

Frying pan意思是油煎的平底锅，字面意思是跳出油煎锅，跳进火坑里。这个习语起源于一个希腊谚语，把情况越来越糟比喻成放在平底锅上油煎的一条活蹦乱跳的鱼，跳出煎锅却掉进了熊熊炉火中。这个比喻非常形像生动，用夸张的手法描绘了逃脱小难，更遭大难；每况愈下。

Fly-by-night
无信誉者

扫码看视频
Scan for video

The store from which I bought this defective alarm clock is terrible. They know they're selling poor quality merchandise. It's an untrustworthy, fly-by-night operation.

我买这个残次品闹钟的商店真是太糟糕了。他们知道他们卖劣质产品。这是不可靠的、无信誉的经营。

Teacher Josh Something that is fly-by-night is not well planned, or unreliable or untrustworthy. It is usually used in reference to business or financial matters. The phrase, which was used initially to insult old women, seems to come from the idea of witches traveling at night on their broomsticks.

Fly-by-night 可不能望文生义，并不是在夜间飞行，但是来源和夜间有关系，女巫师会在夜间骑着他们的扫把飞行，最早的记录是用这个词表示对一个老女人的轻蔑。现在多指没有信用的，不可靠的，特别是在商业或者金融方面。

The early bird gets (catches) the worm

早起的鸟儿有虫吃

扫码看视频
Scan for video

She's always the first one at auctions and that's why she does so well. The early bird gets the worm.

她总是第一个来拍卖交易所，这就是为什么她做得如此好。早起的鸟儿有虫吃。

Teacher Josh This idiom means that someone who begins a task before others has more opportunity and a better chance for success. It comes from the idea that birds that wake up the earliest have the best chance of catching a good meal. This expression was recorded in a book of proverbs by William Camden published in 1605.

The early bird gets (catches) the worm 字面意思是"早起的鸟儿有虫吃"，由于大部分鸟还在熟睡，那么早起的鸟儿抓到虫子的机会是最好的。以此来形容某些人为了抓住某些机会，便会第一个到达或早点到达，成功的机会更高。这个习语首次出现在威廉·卡姆登（William Camden）于1605年写的一本谚语书中。

Word of mouth
口碑

扫码看视频
Scan for video

The new Superman movie has great word of mouth. Apparently, everyone loves it and is telling their friends to see it.

新上映《超人》电影口碑很好。很明显每个人都喜欢并推荐他们的朋友们去看。

Teacher Josh This describes information, usually a review of a product or service, that is passed informally and verbally from person to person. This information can be positive or negative, and it ends up helping other people decide if they want to use the product or service.

Word of mouth 直译是"从嘴巴里说出的单词"，实际意思是用来描述消息是通过人与人之间非正式的口述方式传播，不是写出来而是说出来。如果说某物有好的 word of mouth，意思是人们体验了产品和服务，并把好的体验告诉他们的家人、朋友和陌生人。

City slicker
时髦或世故的城市人

John was timid when he first moved to Manhattan, but after two years he became shrewd, a regular city slicker.

约翰第一次搬到曼哈顿的时候胆小，但是两年后，他变得精明，是一位合格的世故的城市人。

扫码看视频
Scan for video

Teacher Josh A city slicker is a person who lives and works in a metropolis, and is stylish and sophisticated. The term was first used in the early twentieth century. If someone from a rural background calls one a city slicker, it is likely an insult. It implies that people from the city are deceptive, or slick, in some way.

Slicker 意思是骗子，city slicker 是指生活和工作在城市中，比较时髦而且精明世故的人。如果说某人是 city slicker，一般是美国农民对城市人的一种贬低的称呼，正如城市人用 hick 这个词形容乡巴佬一样。据推测这个词首次使用是在1916年，喻指来自城市的人在某些方面上是欺骗的，华而不实。

Catch you later
待会儿见

扫码看视频
Scan for video

I've got to get home for a piano lesson, so I'll speak to you another time — I'll catch you later.

我要回家上一节钢琴课，我晚点和你聊，待会儿见。

Teacher Josh This is an informal way to say goodbye. The expression, which usually implies one is too busy to engage in conversation, was first used by farmers gathering at pubs to chat or drink. When retiring for the night, they would use this phrase to bid farewell to one another.

Catch you later 是另外一种方式说再见。如果某人和你说"catch you later"，暗指他或她目前太忙不能与对方见面或谈话。这是一个古老的习语，农民们在酒吧聚会聊天喝酒，晚上就寝前，他们会彼此告别说"catch you later"，几年后大获流行，现在被很多人使用用来告别。

Wet behind the ears
乳臭未干

扫码看视频
Scan for video

Donald wouldn't hire Greg because he was too young, too inexperienced, too wet behind the ears.

唐纳德不会雇佣格雷格，因为他太年轻了，没有经验，乳臭未干。

Teacher Josh Someone who is wet behind the ears is naïve and inexperienced, usually because he is young. Some say this idiom comes from the idea of human babies who are born wet with amniotic fluid. Others say it refers to newborn farm animals that get licked dry by their mothers; one of the last places to get dried is the area behind the ears.

Wet behind the ears 直译是耳朵后面是湿的，多形容一个人很年轻，幼稚，缺乏经验，初出茅庐，乳臭未干。关于起源有争议。一种说法是说新出生的婴儿来到这个世界上时被羊水液体包围，所以是湿的。另一种说法是新出生的农场动物们，动物妈妈们不得不把新出生的宝贝舔干，最后舔干的地方是耳朵后部。

Too big for your britches
自高自大

I used to like Greg but he's become conceited and haughty. He's too big for his britches.

我曾经喜欢格雷格，但是他已经变得自负与傲慢。他自高自大。

扫码看视频
Scan for video

Teacher Josh A person who is too big for his britches is someone who is too confident or thinks too highly of himself. This idiom, which became popular in the late 1800s, alludes to a person becoming so puffed up with conceit (self-importance) that their pants, or britches, no longer fit.

Britches意思是裤子，"too big for one's britches"意思是一个人变大裤子穿不上了，形容一个人自满自大。这是一个比喻习语，在19世纪末期流行起来。暗喻一个人自满自负，变得膨胀，导致这个人的裤子和靴子不合适。

With flying colors

非常成功地

扫码看视频
Scan for video

Betty passed her math test easily as expected. In fact, she passed with flying colors.

贝蒂轻松地通过了她的数学测试，正如预期结果。事实上，她非常成功地通过了考试。

Teacher Josh

It's good to do something with flying colors as it means it has been done successfully. In this situation, "colors" refer to the flags flown by ships many years ago. When returning after a victory, a ship would sail into a port flying their colors.

如果说做某事 flying colors，指做事很成功。Flying colors 是航海术语，指"迎风飘扬的旗帜"，当一艘战舰和敌舰战争，战舰上的旗帜迎风飘扬的驶入港口，说明战舰没有受到伤害，获得了胜利。

Whole kit and caboodle
全部，一切

扫码看视频
Scan for video

Jimmy bought thirty-one new apps, the fanciest case and two charging cords for his new phone. He wanted it all — the whole kit and caboodle.

吉米为他的新手机买了31个新软件，最时髦的手机壳和两根充电线。他想要全套。

Teacher Josh This saying, which first appeared in the USA in the mid-nineteenth century, likely has military roots. It means a collection of objects, typically tools needed for a job; or the whole lot of something; which can be used to describe items found in a soldier's bag (his kit) of belongings.

Kit是工具箱，caboodle是堆，Whole kit and caboodle指很多东西，全部物品，一套物品。习语首次记载使用是在19世纪中期的美国，习语起源有多种说法，有一种说该习语来自于士兵，士兵作战随身携带一套工具包，这一整套工具包叫做whole kit。

Tongue-in-cheek
开玩笑地

Don't be insulted by what Ted said. He meant it as a joke; it was tongue-in-cheek.

不要被泰德说的话侮辱到。他开玩笑地说。

扫码看视频
Scan for video

Teacher Josh This describes something not meant to be taken seriously, though the speaker is pretending to be serious. It alludes to the michievous facial expression created by pushing the tip of one's tongue against the inside of one's cheek. An early use of this phrase can be found in the novel *The Fair Maid of Perth* (1828), written by Sir Walter Scott.

Tongue-in-cheek 用来形容对某事没必要当真，开玩笑而已。关于它的起源可能来自戏院，演员为了避免笑场，就把舌头伸进腮帮子里。在做鬼脸时通常会把舌头伸到两腮处，很滑稽。书面最早记载源自1828年Walter Scott先生写的《The Fair Maid of Perth》。

Old sins cast long shadows
原罪长久的阴影

扫码看视频
Scan for video

Ned served time in prison years ago and is still paying the price because old sins cast long shadows.

内德因为原罪长久的阴影，几年前在监狱里服刑，现在还在为此付出代价。

Teacher Josh This expression means if one commits a crime or sinful act, one will likely suffer the consequences for a long time. It implies that one should do one's best to be an upstanding, moral human being.

Sins 表示罪行、恶行；cast 表示投射；shadows 表示阴影。这个表达指如果你犯了罪或者做了一些坏事或恶行，你会为此产生的后果遭罪很久。这些罪行会缠着你，对个人影响深远。因此，这个表达暗示人们应该努力成为一名正直的、有道德的人。

Can't hold a candle to
远不如

Steve loves to tap dance, but in relation to Harry he looks like an amateur. Steve can't hold a candle to Harry when it comes to tap dancing.

史蒂夫喜欢踢踏舞，但是和哈里比，他像一名业余爱好者。说到踢踏舞，史蒂夫远不如哈里。

Teacher Josh A person who can't hold a candle to someone or something else is usually inferior. By example: "Jane is pretty but she can't hold a candle to Sophia." This means Sophia is prettier than Jane. In the old days, an apprentice would hold a candle to provide light for the more experienced workman. Someone unable to do the simpler job of holding a candle would be considered lousy.

Candle是蜡烛，所以hold a candle就是手持蜡烛。很多年前还没电灯，是用蜡烛照明的年代。那时学徒工非常期望自己可以给有经验的工人手持蜡烛照明，有一些人甚至连拿蜡烛的资格都没有，这就是习语can't hold a candle to的出典，形容某人或某事低人一等。

Walk on air
非常高兴，得意洋洋

After the doctor told Kate that she was pregnant, she left his office walking on air.

当医生告诉凯特她怀孕了，她特别开心离开了他的办公室，得意洋洋。

Teacher Josh If you are walking on air, you are feeling extremely happy. John Keats, in his romantic poem "Isabella" (1820), used a similar expression to describe two lovers: "Parting they seemed to tread upon the air, twin roses by the zephyr blown apart only to meet again more close."

"Walk on air"并不是在空中走，而是形容一个人非常高兴，得意洋洋，彷佛漫步云端的天使，高兴的飘飘然。英国诗人约翰·济慈（John Keats）在他的浪漫诗《伊莎贝拉》使用类似习语描述两位恋人。诗文这样写道，"Parting they seemed to tread upon the air, Twin roses by the zephyr blown apart only to meet again more closc。"（告别时刻，宛如一对被和风吹散的并蒂玫瑰飘飘然）句中tread upon the air相当于walk on air。

A watched pot never boils

心急吃不了热豆腐

扫码看视频
Scan for video

Waiting in the driveway for Dad to come home isn't going to make him arrive any sooner. A watched pot never boils.

在私家车道上等爸爸回家不会使他很快到来。心急吃不了热豆腐。

Teacher Josh This means that time seems to pass slowly when one is waiting or eager for something to happen. The first use of this idiom was in a report by Benjamin Franklin published in 1785.

Pot是壶，boil是煮，watched pot never boils 是一直看着壶，水却不开，也就是汉语常说的"心急吃不了热豆腐"。当一个人等着某事发生，脑子里只盯着这一件事，时间似乎过得很慢。这个习语首次书面使用源自本杰明·富兰克林1785年发表的一篇报告。

Blow hot and cold
拿不定主意

扫码看视频
Scan for video

Marge blew hot and cold about attending college;
every day she changed her mind.

玛格上大学拿不定主意；每天她都改变想法。

Teacher Josh To blow hot and cold means to alternate between two different or opposite opinions or behaviors — in short, to be uncertain. This is another phrase that originated from *Aesop's Fables*. In one fable, a satyr encounters a traveler who blows his breath upon his hands to warm them, and then blows upon his porridge to cool it off. The satyr is disturbed by how the traveler can do or say opposite things in the same breath.

Blow hot and cold 形容人在两种明显不同的观点、行为、态度等方面犹豫不决，反复变化，拿不定主意。习语出自一则伊索寓言，讲有个人冬天跟森林之神一起吃饭，先是在手上哈气取暖，后来又吹气让热汤凉下来，森林之神因此跟他断绝了关系，认为他反复无常，一会儿嫌冷一会儿嫌热。

In a New York minute
立刻

If I had the money, I'd buy those sneakers as fast as I could. I'd get them in a New York minute!

如果我有钱，我会马上买那些运动鞋，我会立刻得到它们。

扫码看视频
Scan for video

Teacher Josh Surprisingly, this idiom, which means immediately or without hesitation, did not originate in New York. Instead, it is a reflection of how Americans in other parts of the USA view the city as fast-paced. The term was first recorded in the mid-twentieth century in Texas.

In a New York minute 不是纽约分钟，而是指马上，立刻地，毫不犹豫。这个习语不是起源于纽约。相反，这个习语反映了美国其他地区的人们如何看待纽约的生活，和美国其他地区相比，纽约城市的节奏特别快。习语最早记录是在20世纪中期来自德克萨斯州松林区（Piney Woods，Texas）。

Throw in the towel
认输

After Jim took Ted's queen, Ted surrendered; he threw in the towel.

当吉姆战胜泰德的国际象棋皇后，泰德投降了；他认输了。

扫码看视频
Scan for video

Teacher Josh This term comes from boxing and it means to concede defeat or quit voluntarily. When a boxer was unable to continue fighting, someone from his team would throw a towel into the middle of the boxing ring to indicate that the fighter was done fighting.

To throw in the towel 是一个拳击术语，意思是承认失败。在拳击比赛中，教练可以将毛巾投入赛场内，作为停止比赛的信号。在有人放弃或承认失败的情况下，使用这个成语。

White elephant sale
廉价拍卖

Everything that Grandma is selling at her garage sale is useless. It's a white elephant sale if ever there was one.

祖母在车库销售的旧物都没用，廉价拍卖质量很差的产品。

扫码看视频
Scan for video

Teacher Josh

A white elephant sale is a collection of used items for sale. Many of these items are low quality and of little value. The phrase "white elephant" has a different meaning on its own. It refers to something that is costly but of no real use. By example: "The stadium is likely to become a white elephant after the championship is over." This means the stadium will not be used again once the competition ends.

A white elephant sale 指的是卖二手的物品，通常是因为某种原因卖物品募捐。尽管这些物品对某些藏家有用，但是大多数产品是低廉的。大家在使用这个习语的时候千万不要和"white elephant"混淆，"white elephant"指的是非常昂贵而又无用的物品。比如，体育赛事锦标赛结束后留下的体育馆就是一个"white elephant"，因为比赛结束后，没有人会再次使用它。

Square peg in a round hole
格格不入；不适合

I went to the party but I did not know one person and didn't fit in. I felt like a square peg in a round hole.

我参加过一次聚会，但是我不认识任何人，没有融入进去。我感觉自己格格不入。

扫码看视频
Scan for video

Teacher Josh

This is used to describe a situation of a person who is unable to fit into a particular environment or get along with a group of people. In the early 1800s, it was used to describe people whose behavior set them apart from others. Nowadays it is often used to describe someone whose character makes him unsuitable for a job. For example: "He never fit in when he was working here; he was always a bit of a square peg in a round hole."

A square peg in a round hole，直译是将一个方形的钉子放入一个圆形的孔，显然是不合适的，这里指一个人对环境不适应，或者与其他人在一起不舒服。在1800年左右，这个习语用来描述misfits（行为诡异的人），他们的行为和态度通常和社会中其他人不一样。此外，还用来描述某人的个性不适合做某项工作。

Holy Joe

伪装虔诚者；牧师

扫码看视频
Scan for video

Frank makes a show of being morally superior to others — he's a real holy Joe.

佛兰克假装道德上优于其他人，他是一名伪装虔诚者。

Teacher Josh This describes someone who is overly eager to make judgements about the behaviors and choices of others, usually with a sense of being better than them. The term, first recorded in the 1870s, is sometimes used to refer to a minister or priest.

如果我们说某人是"a Holy Joe"，意思是这个人假装虔诚的，自以为是的。但是还有一个简单的意思是"牧师"。这个习语首次记载是在19世纪70年代。

Cool as a cucumber
镇静；自信

Women love Kenny because he's always calm and easy going — he's as cool as a cucumber.

女人们都很喜欢肯尼因为他总是镇静、随和。他镇定自若。

Teacher Josh This expression describes someone who is calm and in control of their feelings in difficult situations. It may have originated from the observation that even in hot weather, the inside of a cucumber remains cool compared to the air. A person who stays relaxed in a difficult situation is unaffected by his surrounding, and thus is figuratively as "cool" as the inside of a cucumber.

As cool as a cucumber 可不是真的和黄瓜一样凉，而是比喻一个人非常地淡定和冷静，镇定自若，能够很好地控制自己的情绪，类似于 calm 的意思。习语最早来自一首诗，18世纪中期一位英国诗人兼剧作家约翰·盖伊（1685～1732）所书写，也许是因为他对黄瓜有所了解或喜好，因为事实上，黄瓜内部的温度的确是是比环境温度要低好几度。一个人身处困境依然镇定自若，内部的平静可以用 as cool as a cucumber 来形容。

In good part
很大程度上；欣然地

Our team's victory is in good part due to our great coach.

我们团队取得的胜利很大程度上是因为我们伟大的教练。

Teacher Josh

This expression has two meanings. Most commonly, it means "to a large extent." By example: "Her fluency in English is in good part due to her diligent study." It also means to respond without offense or in good humor. By example: "My friends tease me about my passion for rubber ducks, but I've learned to take it in good part."

"In good part"有两个意思。最常用的意思是"很大程度上"，比如说"Her fluency in English is in good part due to diligent study。"（她的英语流利度很大程度上取决于努力学习。）第二个意思是对某事欣然接受，或不在意无所谓，比如"My friends tease me about my passion for rubber ducks, but I've learned to take it in good part。"（我朋友取笑我钟爱橡皮鸭子，但是我不在意。）意思是我不会因为他们取笑我而生气，并没有使我恼怒。

Hold your horses
不要着急

Patty was yanking her father by the hand toward the line for the carousel. As he felt that she was running too quickly, he told her, "Hold your horses."

帕蒂用力拽着她爸爸的手朝旋转木马奔去。她爸爸觉着帕蒂跑的太快，对她说："不要着急。"

Teacher Josh

This is a way of telling someone to wait or stop. The term originated from a time when transportation by horses was common. A driver of a horse-drawn vehicle might be asked to hold his horses still so that the customer may board the carriage safely.

Hold your horses 直译是"拴住你的马"，过去，马是主要的交通工具，人们在骑马或乘坐马车前会对骑手说"Hold your horses"，然后再上马车或骑马。如果你在气头上，别人可能会跟你说："Hold your horses。"他想表达的意思是"沉住气，别冒火。"所以hold one's horses表示暂停暂缓，不着急行事。

Blue in the face
非常生气

扫码看视频
Scan for video

She asked the guard to unlock her cell over and over again, but the guard said she could ask until she was blue in the face and he still wouldn't open it.

她一遍又一遍地请求警卫打开她的房门，但是警卫说她非常生气地要求，他也不会开门。

Teacher Josh

A person who is blue in the face is exhausted or frustrated from being angry or trying to do something with no results. This expression alludes to the bluish color that the skin takes on when one has a lack of oxygen, which can result from arguing or talking until one is breathless. This is used to refer to someone fuming with rage.

Blue in the face 字面意思"脸变蓝了"，一个人非常生气，一直说话，说的缺氧，脸色发青。引申为"脸色发青，面红耳赤，气的要命并且徒劳无功"，常用搭配"till/until one is blue in the face"。如果你只是一般的生气，不可以使用这个习语，但是如果你是非常生气的，当然可以使用。

Out of one's element
处于不适宜的环境

Nick felt like he did not belong in the gym, that he was out of his element, because he was so out of shape.

尼克感觉自己不属于健身房，他不适合这个环境，因为他身材走形了。

扫码看视频
Scan for video

Teacher Josh

When you are out of your element, you are in an environment that is unfamiliar and uncomfortable, or that you are not suited for, much like a fish out of water. The term element refers to the concept of earth, water, air and fire as the natural environment of living things. When one is out of one's element, one is not good at or does not enjoy doing something.

To feel out of one's element 意思是感觉不舒服，就像鱼离开水一样。习语中的element是指的四个元素：土、水、空气和火，这四元素是生物居住必备的。如果说"you are out of your element"，意思是你不擅长做某事，比如"Teacher Josh is in his element teaching。He hopes his students are in their element learning to speak English with idioms from the streets of New York!"（Josh老师擅长教学。他希望他的学生说英语时擅长使用来自纽约街头的习语。）

Keep a stiff upper lip
保持镇静自若

EMERGENCY ROOM

扫码看视频
Scan for video

John was worried about his daughter's illness, but he tried to hide his concern from the rest of the family — he tried to keep a stiff upper lip.

约翰很担心他女儿的病情，但是他尽力不对家庭其他成员显示他的忧虑，他保持镇静自若。

Teacher Josh

This idiom means to appear as if you are not upset when facing difficulties or misfortune. It originated in the USA in the early 1800s, and makes reference to one's upper lip that trembles when one is about to cry. To keep a stiff upper lip therefore means you do your best to prevent your lip from trembling and any negative emotion from showing.

Stiff，指绷紧不动的，所以 keep a stiff upper lip直译：绷紧上唇保持不动。习语起源于19世纪的美国，我们知道处于危急情势而万分惊恐的人嘴唇往往会不由自主地哆嗦。忧伤悲痛强忍眼泪的人有时双唇也会抖动。在1830年的时候，美国男士几乎人人都留八字胡，这就使上唇的抖动更显眼。难怪人们要费劲地保持上唇不动，来掩饰自己的惊慌或悲痛。

Index

Josh Bobley, known as Teacher Josh, was born and raised in New York. He is a renowned educator based in Shanghai. His expertise is English language instruction; journalism; and public speaking, which he teaches to students ranging in age from five to fifty.

He offers classes at various local schools, provides private tutorials and is frequently invited to host major events at museums and government-sponsored events, including a national English language competition for young journalists honing their skills in preparation for the 2022 Beijing Winter Games. He has tens of thousands of followers on his English studies page on KuaiShou (快手), a popular social media site in China.

Since his first trip to China in 1981, Josh has been keenly interested in its language and culture, and speaks fluent Mandarin. He holds a master's degree in Chinese studies from Yale (1991) and a master's from Columbia University's School of Journalism (1998). He is an accomplished classical pianist, having studied at the Manhattan School of Music, and has made several recordings of his interpretations of J.S. Bach, his favorite composer.

Mingxia Ma, 马铭霞, is a bilingual educator born and raised in Weifang, China, and currently teaches hospitality management at Shandong Vocational College of Economics and Business. Ms. Ma holds a bachelor of arts degree in English literature from Qingdao University, a second bachelor's in business from IMC Fachhochschule Krems (University of Applied Science) in Austria, and a master's in Business Management from Bohai University. She translated this book's English explanations to Chinese.

Having traveled to the US several times, where she worked and studied, she has been interested in American culture for many years, and is equally interested in Chinese history, art and literature. Ms. Ma is a connoisseur of Chinese cuisine and prides herself on her knowledge of the traditional Chinese tea ceremony.

Peter A Bobley is a 76-year-old entrepreneur, author and Broadway play producer. He lives on Long Island, New York, with his wife. He has five children and five grandchildren. Peter has been a copywriter for 50 years and has written hundreds of commercials and brochures. He is known for the way he employs punchy, New York language and idioms. He is the author of two books, *Nobody Asked Me, But…* and *"Mom, We're Black!": Humankind's Journey*. He produced *The First* on Broadway, a musical biography of Jackie Robinson, the first black baseball player to play in the major leagues.

Patrick Carlson is a cartoonist and illustrator from Valdosta, GA. He discovered his love for drawing as a child and began freelancing in college. With a degree in early childhood education, Patrick used his experience in teaching to create cartoons and illustrations for logos, apparel and children's books. In 2004, Patrick quit his teaching position, created bbqlogos.com, and began a full-time career as a cartoonist and illustrator. Today, he has illustrated dozens of children's books and thousands of cartoons for businesses and logos around the world. He lives with his wife, Jennifer, and twin sons, Alex and Ben.